the
FLEXITARIAN
COOKBOOK

ADAPTABLE RECIPES FOR PART-TIME
VEGETARIANS AND VEGANS

Compiled by
JULIA CHARLES

SENIOR DESIGNER Toni Kay
HEAD OF PRODUCTION
  Patricia Harrington
ART DIRECTOR Leslie Harrington
EDITORIAL DIRECTOR Julia Charles
PUBLISHER Cindy Richards
INDEXER Hilary Bird
ILLUSTRATOR Harriet Popham

First published in 2019 by
Ryland Peters & Small
20–21 Jockey's Fields
London WC1R 4BW
and 341 E 116th St
New York NY 10029
www.rylandpeters.com

This edition published in South Africa
in 2019 by Struik Lifestyle,
an imprint of Penguin Random House
South Africa (Pty) Ltd
Company Reg. No. 1953/000441/07
The Estuaries, 4 Oxbow Crescent,
Century Avenue, Century City 7441
PO Box 1144, Cape Town, 8000,
South Africa
www.penguinrandomhouse.co.za

ISBN: 978-1-43231-076-9

Printed and bound in China

Reprinted in 2020

Recipe collection and flexitarian
variations devised by Julia Charles.
Original recipe text copyright ©
Chloe Coker, Ross Dobson, Amy Ruth
Finegold, Mat Follas, Liz Franklin,
Dunja Gulin, Vicky Jones, Jenny
Linford, Jane Montgomery, Louise
Pickford, Jenny Tschiesche, Leah
Vanderveldt and Belinda Williams
2019. See page 144 for full credits.

Design and photography ©
Ryland Peters & Small 2019.
Illustrations © Harriet Popham 2019.

Notes:
• Both British (Metric) and American (Imperial
plus US cups) measurements are included in
these recipes for your convenience, however it
is important to work with one set of
measurements and not alternate between
the two within a recipe.
• All spoon measurements are level unless
otherwise specified.
• When a recipe calls for the grated zest
of citrus fruit, buy unwaxed fruit.
• Cheeses started with animal rennet are
not suitable for vegetarians so read food
labelling carefully and check that any cheese
you are using is made with a non-animal
(microbial) starter. Traditional Parmesan
is not vegetarian so where vegetarian
Parmesan is specified in these recipes we
recommend finding a vegetarian hard cheese
which has the same texture as Parmesan
and is therefore suitable for grating.

CONTENTS

INTRODUCTION

Today many of us are looking to eat less dairy, meat and fish, as the host of environmental, ethical and health-related reasons for doing so stacks up. The concept of not centring every meal around an animal-based protein is well on its way to settling into mainstream society but out there, there is a whole middle-ground of home-cooks, placed somewhere between carnivore and vegan, who are doing their best to reduce meat and fish consumption, but enjoying it on occasion when the urge strikes. For these so-called flexitarians, choices are less about adopting a rigid regime, and more about an organic attempt to eat a mainly plant-based diet.

This timely cookbook is a collection of modern recipes and comfort food classics, all of which feature simple adaptations that can make them suitable for vegans, vegetarians, pescatarians and meat-eaters. So as an aspiring flexitarian, you can simply choose the dairy, meat or fish option as the mood or occasion takes you. No longer will you have to juggle between multiple cookbooks or haphazardly hash together a meaty ending to a recipe depending on your appetite or cravings!

All recipes and available variations feature symbols indicating which dietary choice they suit, as follows:

V Vegetarian – *excludes meat, fish and poultry but includes eggs and all dairy products, however cheeses should be vegetarian (see right and note on page 4).*

VE Vegan – *excludes meat, fish and poultry as Vegetarian (but also excludes eggs, all dairy products and honey.*

PE Pescatarian – *as Vegetarian but also includes fish and seafood.*

M Meat-eater – *includes meat, fish, poultry, eggs, all dairy products (including rennet-started cheeses) and honey.*

Either cook the main recipe as shown or choose one of the adaptations on offer to create the perfect dish for your dietary requirements, as well as something that you really fancy eating. Some recipes can be portioned and adjusted during cooking and finished or served to suit two different dietary requirements – a very useful feature if you are cooking for the family or a group of friends and have more than one need to cater for. Recipes to enjoy include a Borlotti Bean & Fennel Stew with the option to include pork shoulder; a delicious Mushroom & Bean Chili Sin Carne that reinvents itself with chunks of beef; Tangy Tomato Tacos with Guacamole that turn into Spicy Turkey Tacos; and a dairy-free Beetroot/beet Risotto that also works with the addition of crumbled feta and fresh mint or even smoked mackerel and horseradish cream.

Basic recipes for a Vegan Cheese, Vegan Parmesan and Vegan Cream are included (see page 8) for your convenience but shopping for dairy substitutes has never been easier (or more exciting!) so check out your local supermarket (or look online) for new products. Be aware that quite a number of traditional cheeses (including Parmesan, Pecorino, Manchego, Gruyère, Gorgonzola and Roquefort) are not suitable for vegetarians as they have been started with rennet (an enzyme of animal origin) so read the packaging carefully. Some brands now make and sell these cheese styles using vegetarian-friendly alternatives, but you will need to look for them. Dairy-free vegan cheeses (often nut-based) are now more readily available than ever before so again, look out for new products to try. Dairy-free milks and creams made from soy, rice and oats are all plentiful so try some different types and use what you most enjoy. These recipes mostly make use of beans and pulses/legumes as the protein source for a plant-based diet but on a few occasions mock meat substitutes are suggested, so again, shop around to find an (ideally) organic and additive-free brand that you enjoy – health-food stores are a good place to start.

Lastly, all of the key ingredients in the recipe adaptations (as well as the main recipes) are indexed on pages 142–143 so make use of this if you are looking specifically for a meal containing tofu, cod, prawns/shrimp, chicken, lamb or beef and so on. It's time to liberate the flexitarian cook inside you and become a kitchen alchemist with this ingenious book!

VEGAN CHEESE

400-g/14-oz can chopped
    tomatoes
300 g/2½ cups unroasted
    cashew nuts
4 teaspoons dark miso
    paste
50 g/3½ tablespoons dried
    onions
½ teaspoon salt
50 ml/3½ tablespoons
    sherry vinegar
1 teaspoon Dijon mustard
1 dash of Tabasco sauce
50 ml/3½ tablespoons
    unrefined coconut oil

MAKES 1¾ LB/28 OZ.

There are many vegan cheeses available that use nuts to provide a similar texture to dairy cheese but they can lack flavour. This is a great cheese to eat. It works well in place of cheese for cooking, or serve on its own.

Add all the ingredients, except the coconut oil, to a saucepan, set over a low heat and bring to a low simmer. Stir to combine, then leave in the fridge overnight.

Transfer the mixture to a food processor and purée until smooth. Slowly add the coconut oil, then continue to blend until the mixture is combined and smooth.

Press the mixture into a non-reactive container and chill in the fridge for at least 4 hours until firm. Substitute for dairy cheese.

VEGAN PARMESAN

150 g/1¼ cups unroasted
    cashews
¼ teaspoon garlic powder
4 tablespoons nutritional
    yeast
1 teaspoon salt

MAKES 170 G/6 OZ.

Traditional Parmesan uses animal rennet in the formation of the cheese as well as dairy milk, so this makes a good replacement.

Place all the ingredients in a small food processor and blitz until it becomes a coarse powder. Transfer to an airtight container and store in the cupboard for up to 1 week. This can be used in place of a sprinkle of Parmesan in any of the vegan or vegetarian recipes in this book that require it.

VEGAN CREAM

¼ teaspoon xanthan gum
3 teaspoons rice flour
150 g/1¼ cups unroasted
    cashew nuts, softened
    overnight in water

MAKES 150 ML/5 OZ.

This substitute for dairy cream has a good flavour. Xantham gum is available in supermarkets, usually in the gluten-free or baking section.

Pour 200 ml/¾ cup of water into a saucepan, set over a medium heat and bring to the boil. Pour into a food processor and start the motor.

Add the xanthan gum and rice flour, then slowly add the cashew nuts. Blend to a smooth cream.

Cool, then chill in the fridge for a few hours. Keep refrigerated for up to 4 days, or freeze in an ice cube tray for later use.

BREAKFAST
& BRUNCH

BREAKFAST MUFFINS

These muffins are a fantastic grab-and-go midweek breakfast and make a good substitute for jam/jelly on toast when you don't have time to sit down. They also make the kitchen smell wonderful as they bake!

200 g/1½ cups plain/
  all-purpose flour
60 g/½ cup plain
  wholemeal/whole-wheat
  flour
2½ teaspoons baking
  powder
¼ teaspoon salt
½ teaspoons ground
  cinnamon
300 ml/1¼ cups plain
  soy milk
130 g/½ cup brown rice
  syrup
100 g/½ cup coconut oil
freshly squeezed juice and
  grated zest of 1 lemon
1 small apple, peeled,
  cored and diced
60 g/½ cup raisins
100 g/4 tablespoons firm
  apricot jam/jelly
50 g/½ cup chopped pecans

12-hole muffin pan, lined
  with muffin cases

MAKES 9–12

Preheat the oven to 180°C (350°F) Gas 4.

Sift together the flours, baking powder, salt and cinnamon in a bowl and mix well. In a separate bowl, mix together the milk, syrup, oil, lemon juice and zest.

Combine both bowls and mix gently with a silicone spatula. Do not overmix. Add the apples and raisins and gently mix in.

Fill the muffin cases half-full with the mixture, then put 1 full teaspoon of jam/jelly on top. Cover each one with more of the cake mixture, making sure you fill the cases only three-quarters full. If you have any cake mixture left, repeat this process in further muffin cases until you run out of mixture. Top with a sprinkle of chopped pecans for extra texture.

Bake in the preheated oven for 30 minutes or until golden. Remove from the muffin pan and allow to cool on a wire rack.

V CHEESECAKE MUFFINS Prepare the muffins as above but omit the raisins and add 1 teaspoon of full-fat cream cheese along with the jam/jelly. Bake as the main recipe. The baked muffin will break open to reveal a delicious jam/jelly rippled cream cheese filling.

GRAIN-FREE GRANOLA VE

Granola gets a bad name for being full of sugar. This tasty and nutritious granola uses natural sugars and even forgoes the grains to make it more filling. This means that you need less of it and you can layer it with yogurt and berries in glasses for a delicious and rather visually impressive breakfast.

50 g/5 tablespoons coconut oil, melted
65 g/¼ cup maple syrup
100 g/2 cups dried coconut chips or flakes
100 g/1 cup chopped nuts and/or seeds
½ teaspoon ground cinnamon
handful of dried fruit

baking sheet, lined with baking parchment

SERVES 3

Preheat the oven to 190°C (375°F) Gas 5.

Mix the melted coconut oil and maple syrup together in a small bowl.

Put the coconut chips or flakes, nuts/seeds, cinnamon and dried fruit in a large bowl and mix together. Pour the coconut oil/maple syrup mixture over the dry ingredients and mix well.

Spread the granola out over the lined baking sheet. Bake in the preheated oven for 15–20 minutes until starting to brown, stirring twice during cooking time. Keep a close eye on it, as it will burn easily. Remove from the oven and leave to cool before serving.

V YOGURT, BERRY & GRANOLA PARFAITS Add a low-fat natural/plain yogurt (such as Skyr or 0–2% Greek yogurt) and a punnet of mixed fresh berries, such as strawberries, raspberries and blueberries. Build layered parfaits in sundae glasses by spooning a tablespoon of the granola into each glass and follow with 2 tablespoons of yogurt and then 2 more of berries. Repeat and top with a sprinkle of granola and a drizzle of maple syrup or honey.

BAKED OAT MILK PORRIDGE
WITH PEARS, ALMONDS & DATE SYRUP

Oven-baking porridge means that you can swap standing at the hob and stirring constantly for simply mixing everything together and leaving it to morph into breakfast heaven under its own steam.

160 g/1¾ cups jumbo oats

1.2 litres/5 cups oat milk, plus extra to serve

75 g/½ cup mixed seeds

2 teaspoons vanilla bean paste

1 teaspoon ground cinnamon

3 medium ripe, but firm pears, cored and diced

80 g/⅔ cup mixed dried berries (sultanas/ golden raisins, goji berries, golden berries, cranberries, etc.)

2 tablespoons toasted flaked/slivered almonds, to serve

4–5 tablespoons date syrup, to serve

extra oat milk, to serve

SERVES 4–6

Preheat the oven to 170°C (325°F) Gas 3.

Mix the oats and oat milk together. Stir in the seeds, vanilla bean paste, ground cinnamon, diced pears and dried berries. Pour everything into a roasting pan, cover with foil and bake for 30 minutes. Remove from the oven and spoon into bowls. Scatter with the toasted almonds and drizzle with date syrup and extra oat milk as desired. Serve at once.

___ ___ ___ ___ ___ ___ ___ ___ ___ ___

V BAKED MILK PORRIDGE WITH PEACHES, HAZELNUTS & HONEY
Replace the oat milk with dairy milk, the pears with peaches, the almonds with roughly chopped hazelnuts and the date syrup with runny honey in the same quantities and follow the main recipe. Serve with extra milk, if liked.

___ ___ ___ ___ ___ ___ ___ ___ ___ ___

TOFU SCRAMBLE VE

This tasty way of using tofu looks and tastes very similar to scrambled eggs. You can use many different vegetables, herbs and spices to ring the changes and this is just one suggestion for springtime, when asparagus (wild and cultivated) is available at farmers' markets. Use a big cast-iron wok to make this dish, or you can also use a heavy-bottomed frying pan/skillet.

150 g/2 cups fresh shiitake mushrooms
4 tablespoons olive oil
120 g/1 cup onions sliced into thin half-moons
½ teaspoon sea salt
80 g/1 cup trimmed asparagus, sliced diagonally at the bottom (if using wild asparagus, then only use the soft tops)
2 tablespoons tamari
½ teaspoon ground turmeric
300 g/10 oz. fresh tofu, mashed with a fork
1 teaspoon dark sesame oil
½ teaspoon dried basil or 2 tablespoons freshly chopped fresh basil
freshly ground black pepper

SERVES 2–3

Cut the mushrooms in half lengthways, then cut into thinner wedges. Add the olive oil, onions and salt to the wok or frying pan/skillet and sauté over a medium heat briefly, stirring energetically to prevent sticking.

Add the mushrooms, asparagus, tamari and turmeric and continue stirring with two wooden spoons. When the mushrooms have soaked up a bit of tamari, turn up the heat, add the tofu and stir for another 1–2 minutes. The scramble should be uniformly yellow in colour. At this point you can add up to 4 tablespoons water to make the scramble juicy, and continue cooking for a couple more minutes. However, whether you need water or not depends on how soft your tofu was to begin with – softer types are moist and don't need any water at the end of cooking.

Mix in the dark sesame oil and basil, season with pepper and serve warm, with a nice salad and a few slices of toasted homemade bread.

V SUNDRIED TOMATO & GOAT'S CHEESE TOFU SCRAMBLE Omit the asparagus and mushrooms and replace with 6 sun-dried tomatoes, sliced, and 80 g/3 oz. soft goat's cheese, cut into pieces. Add these with the tamari and turmeric to the pan and finish as main recipe.

EGGS EN COCOTTE
WITH MUSHROOMS

1 tablespoon olive oil

½ onion, finely chopped

400 g/14 oz. white/
  cup mushrooms,
  thinly sliced

2 tablespoons freshly
  chopped tarragon leaves,
  plus extra to garnish

4 eggs

4 tablespoons double/
  heavy cream

4 tablespoons grated
  vegetarian Parmesan
  cheese

salt and freshly ground
  black pepper

4 *ramekins*

SERVES 4

Mushrooms and eggs have a delicious affinity – their delicate flavours complementing each other, rather than overpowering, so this traditional comfort dish is given a luxurious touch by adding a layer of fried mushrooms. A hint of tarragon adds a pleasing aniseed note. Serve with toast fingers for a satisfying brunch.

Preheat the oven to 180°C (350°F) Gas 4.

Heat the olive oil in a frying pan/skillet. Fry the onion over a low heat, until softened. Add the mushrooms, increase the heat, and fry briefly until the mushrooms are softened. Mix in the tarragon, season with salt and freshly ground black pepper, and cook for a further 2 minutes.

Divide the mushroom mixture between the 4 ramekin dishes. Break an egg into the centre of each ramekin. Season the eggs with salt and freshly ground black pepper. Pour a tablespoon of double/heavy cream over each egg, then sprinkle each with vegetarian Parmesan cheese.

Bake in the preheated oven for 8–10 minutes for runny yolks, or 15–20 minutes for set yolks. Garnish with tarragon and serve warm from the oven.

M HAM, MUSHROOM & EGG RAMEKINS Omit the onions and replace with 100 g/4 oz. of finely diced uncured ham. Sauté the ham in the frying pan/skillet with the mushrooms until everything is browned. Mix in the tarragon, season with salt and pepper and divide between 4 ramekins. Finish as main recipe, using regular Parmesan if liked.

TUNISIAN BAKED EGGS

This classic North African dish (shakshuka) is now hugely popular as a brunch option in cafés but also very easy to make at home. Serve with plenty of crusty bread for mopping up the spiced tomato sauce.

450 g/1 lb. ripe tomatoes
1 tablespoon olive oil
1 onion, chopped
1 red (bell) pepper, chopped into strips
1 garlic clove, chopped
1 teaspoon ground cumin
½ teaspoon harissa
1 teaspoon brown sugar
4 eggs
freshly chopped coriander/cilantro, to garnish
salt and freshly ground black pepper

SERVES 4

Roughly chop the tomatoes, reserving the juices.

Heat the olive oil in a large, heavy-bottomed frying pan/skillet set over a medium heat. Add the onion, (bell) pepper and garlic and fry, stirring often, for 5 minutes, until softened.

Mix the cumin with 1 tablespoon of water in a small bowl to form a paste.

Add the harissa and cumin paste to the pan and fry, stirring, for a minute. Add the tomatoes and brown sugar, season with salt and pepper, and mix well. Bring to the boil, reduce the heat, cover and simmer for 5 minutes.

Uncover and simmer for a further 10 minutes, stirring now and then, to reduce and thicken the tomato mixture.

Break the eggs, spaced well apart, into the tomato mixture. Cover and cook over a low heat for 10 minutes until the eggs are set.

Sprinkle with coriander/cilantro and serve at once.

VE CHICKPEA & TOFU SHAKSHUKA Omit the eggs and replace with 300 g/2 cups cooked chickpeas and 350 g/12 oz. firm silken tofu. Carefully slice the block of tofu in half lengthways, so that you have 2 thinner blocks. Using a cookie cutter, cut out 2 rounds from each block and set aside. (Reserve the leftover tofu to use in soups or smoothies). Follow as main recipe, adding the chickpeas for the last 5 minutes of simmering just to warm them through. Next, arrange the tofu rounds on top of the mixture in the frying pan/skillet and finish as main recipe. To add flavour, dust the tofu lightly with baharat spice mix before serving.

SEEDED BAKED PANCAKE
WITH BERRIES & RAW COCOA SAUCE

PANCAKE BATTER
50 g/generous ⅓ cup
 plain/all-purpose flour
3 tablespoons coconut flour
1 teaspoon baking powder
pinch of salt
150 ml/⅔ cup milk
3 eggs, beaten
4 tablespoons runny honey
1 teaspoon pure vanilla
 extract
5 tablespoons mixed seeds,
 such as linseeds/
 flaxseeds, chia seeds,
 sunflower seeds, poppy
 seeds
2 tablespoons coconut oil

COCOA SAUCE
4 tablespoons raw cocoa
 powder
2½ tablespoons runny
 honey
2½ tablespoons coconut oil,
 melted

TO SERVE
150 g/¾ cup Greek yogurt
50 g/1¾ oz. dried berries,
 such as goji, acai,
 cranberries etc.
100 g/3½ oz. mixed fresh
 berries such as
 blueberries, raspberries,
 redcurrants etc.
icing/confectioners' sugar

*22-cm/9-inch ovenproof
 frying pan/skillet*

SERVES 4

Based on the Dutch-style pancake that is baked in the oven, this is a super-easy and delicious way to make a pancake to serve straight from the pan. This recipe is packed full of nutritious seeds and served with fresh berries and a delicious cocoa sauce for a truly indulgent but power-packed breakfast.

Preheat the oven to 200°C (400°F) Gas 6.

To make the pancakes, sift the plain/all-purpose flour, coconut flour, baking powder and salt into a mixing bowl. Combine the milk, eggs, honey and vanilla in a separate bowl and beat into the flours to make a smooth batter. Fold in the mixed seeds.

Heat the coconut oil in the ovenproof frying pan/skillet until melted. Pour in the pancake batter and transfer to the oven. Bake in the preheated oven for 15 minutes until the pancake is puffed up and golden.

Meanwhile, make the cocoa sauce. Place all the ingredients with 4 tablespoons water in a saucepan and heat gently, stirring, until smooth. Keep warm.

As soon as the pancake is cooked, remove it from the oven. Spoon the yogurt into the centre and top with the dried and fresh berries. Drizzle over the cocoa sauce and serve dusted with icing/confectioners' sugar.

VE DUTCH PANCAKE WITH BERRIES & COCOA SAUCE Omit the Pancake Batter and replace with an unseeded vegan batter, as follows: Melt 1½ tablespoons of vegan butter substitute and pour into a food processor. Add 125 ml/½ cup almond milk, 285 g/10 oz. silken soft tofu, 90 ml/⅓ cup maple syrup, 1½ teaspoons pure vanilla extract, 60 ml/¼ cup freshly squeezed orange juice and blend on medium-high speed. Add 135 g/1 cup plain/all-purpose flour and a pinch of salt and blend again until lump-free and smooth. Let rest for 10–20 minutes before using. Heat 1½ tablespoons of vegan butter substitute in a pan and pour in the rested batter. Bake in an oven preheated to 170°C (350° F) Gas 4 for 30–35 minutes. Finish as main recipe, substituting a thick coconut yogurt for the Greek yogurt.

SNACKS & LIGHTER PLATES

CHICKPEA SOCCA PANCAKES
WITH MUSHROOMS & THYME VE

Socca are crispy-edged Mediterranean pancakes made with chickpea (gram) flour, which makes them gluten-free. They are perfect for topping with savoury or sweet ingredients. Slightly thicker than crepes, socca have a nutty-sweet flavour and a high protein content, which makes them more of a wholesome, filling meal.

125 g/1 cup chickpea
   (gram) flour
½ teaspoon salt
olive oil, for frying

MUSHROOMS
1 tablespoon olive oil
5 fresh thyme sprigs, leaves
   removed from the stems
225 g/8 oz. chestnut/
   cremini mushrooms,
   sliced
1 garlic clove, crushed
salt and freshly ground
   black pepper

SERVES 2

Put the chickpea (gram) flour, salt and 295 ml/1¼ cups water into a large bowl and mix together with a whisk to make a smooth batter. Leave to stand at room temperature for at least 10 minutes.

Meanwhile, heat a thin layer of oil in a large frying pan/skillet over a high heat. Add the thyme leaves and mushrooms and cook, stirring occasionally, for 2–3 minutes until the mushrooms soften and are slightly golden. Reduce the heat to medium, then add the garlic and cook for 1 minute more. Season to taste with salt and pepper. Keep the mushrooms warm in a low oven or in a covered dish while you cook the pancakes.

Heat the olive oil in another small frying pan/skillet over a medium heat. Add approximately 60–75 ml/¼ – scant ⅓ cup of the socca batter to the warm pan. Swirl it around so that it covers the base of the pan. Fry for about 2–3 minutes, until the batter begins to form bubbles. Flip with a spatula and cook for another 1–2 minutes on the other side.

Repeat with the remaining batter to make 4 small socca.

V SOCCA WITH SCRAMBLED EGGS & ROASTED TOMATOES Prepare the socca as main recipe. Roast about 140 g/5 oz. of on-the-vine cherry tomatoes (on a non-stick baking sheet) in an oven preheated to 180°C (350°F) Gas 4 for about 10 minutes, until soft and releasing their juices. Meanwhile, add a knob/pat of butter to a non-stick saucepan and add 4 beaten and seasoned eggs with splash of milk. Scramble over a medium heat, stirring continuously. Spoon the eggs over the warm socca, top with a stem of tomatoes, a little freshly chopped flat-leaf parsley and a grinding of black pepper.

PE CHICKPEA SOCCA WITH SMOKED SALMON & AVOCADO Prepare the socca as main recipe. Top each warm pancake with slices of about 50 g/2 oz. of smoked salmon and slices of fresh avocado. Squeeze over some lemon juice, add a sprinkle of freshly snipped chives and a grinding of black pepper.

TANGY TOMATO TACOS
WITH GUACAMOLE VE

There is a wonderful balance between the crunch of the tacos, spicy heat of the tomatoes and coolness of the guacamole here. Add some spiced up minced/ground turkey to turn them into a meaty-licious meal.

300 g/2 cups cherry tomatoes, quartered
small bunch of fresh coriander/cilantro, finely chopped
grated zest of 1 lime
2 teaspoons white wine vinegar
2 jalapeño chillies/chiles, thinly sliced
1–2 teaspoons cayenne pepper, to season, plus extra to serve
salt

GUACAMOLE
2 large avocados
freshly squeezed juice of 1 lime
small bunch of fresh coriander/cilantro, roughly chopped
1 garlic clove, crushed
1 red onion, finely diced

TO SERVE
8 taco shells
Vegan Cream (see page 8), or any non-dairy cream, or sour cream for a vegetarian option

SERVES 4

To make the tomato salad, mix all the ingredients together in a large mixing bowl, adding cayenne pepper to taste; just 1 teaspoon of cayenne pepper makes a nice, moderately hot salad. Finish with a generous pinch of salt.

To make the guacamole, cut the avocados in half using a small, sharp knife. Remove the pit, scoop out the flesh and roughly chop. Mix in the lime juice immediately to stop it discolouring. Add the coriander/cilantro, garlic and onion, mix all the ingredients together and mash a little using a fork to achieve a rough texture.

Serve the salad with the guacamole at the table, with taco shells and sour cream on the side, or build the tacos by putting a large spoonful of the tomato salad in each one, then a similar amount of the guacamole on top. Finish with a dollop of vegan cream and a sprinkle of cayenne pepper.

M **SPICY TURKEY TACOS** Replace the tomato salad with spicy minced/ground turkey. Heat 1 tablespoon oil in a large frying pan/skillet. Add 1 finely chopped onion and cook until softened. Add 2 crushed garlic cloves and 2 teaspoons each hot smoked paprika and ground cumin and cook for about 30 seconds. Add 450 g/1 lb. minced/ground turkey and cook for 2 minutes. Add 200 g/7 oz. passata/strained tomatoes, 2 teaspoons cider vinegar and 1 teaspoon brown sugar. Simmer for about 4 minutes, or until the turkey is cooked. Season to taste and serve on the table in place of the tomato salad, along with the taco shells, guacamole and sour cream, but omit the cayenne pepper.

SALT-BAKED BEETROOT & MANGO WITH NERIGOMA DRESSING VE

Salt-baking seems to intensify the sweetness of beetroot/beet. If you can manage to find different coloured beetroots/beets, it makes this an even more beautiful dish. Served here in little lettuce cups, it makes a very attractive light meal or appetizer.

800 g/4 cups coarse sea salt
3 egg whites
4 candy-striped and yellow beetroots/beets
50 ml/3½ tablespoons olive oil
freshly squeezed juice of 2 limes
1 teaspoon caster/granulated sugar
1 small red onion, sliced
1 large ripe tomato, roughly chopped
1 medium, ripe mango, peeled, pitted and diced
small handful of freshly chopped coriander/cilantro
salt and freshly ground black pepper
Little Gem lettuce
fresh mint leaves, to garnish

NERIGOMA DRESSING
4 tablespoons nerigoma
zest and juice of 1 lime
1 large garlic clove, finely grated

baking sheet, lined with baking parchment

SERVES 4

Preheat the oven to 190°C (375°F) Gas 5.

Put the salt into a large bowl and mix in the egg whites. Spread about a third of the mixture in a thin layer on the lined baking sheet. Place the beetroots/beets close together, and then pat the remaining salt mixture over the beetroots/beets to cover them. Bake for about 1 hour, until the beetroots/beets are soft when tested with the point of a knife.

Meanwhile, mix the olive oil, lime juice and sugar in a large bowl. Season with salt and pepper.

When the beetroots/beets are cooked, give the salt crusts a thwack with a rolling pin, and remove them. Once the beetroots/beets are cool enough, gently peel away the skin and cut them into dice. Drop them into the lime juice mixture whilst they are still warm, and leave to cool completely. Add the onion, tomato and mango to the bowl and stir in the chopped coriander/cilantro.

Whisk all the ingredients for the nerigoma dressing together with 3–4 tablespoons water. Carefully peel away layers of the lettuce to make cups and fill them with the beetroot/beet mixture. Garnish with mint leaves, and serve with the nerigoma dressing.

V SALT-BAKED BEETROOT, FETA & ENDIVE WITH WALNUT DRESSING
Prepare the beetroot following the main recipe. When dressing, substitute lemon juice for lime, omit the coriander/cilantro and replace the mango with 100 g/3½ oz. of cubed feta cheese. Omit the Nerigoma Dressing and instead whisk 1 tablespoon sherry vinegar, 1 teaspoon balsamic vinegar, ½ teaspoon Dijon mustard, 1 crushed garlic clove, 3 tablespoons olive oil and 1 tablespoon walnut oil until emulsified. Serve in Belgian endive cups with the walnut dressing.

PE PRAWN/SHRIMP & MANGO ICEBERG CUPS Follow the main recipe but halve the quantity of mango and replace with 100 g/3½ oz. peeled and cooked small, sweet prawns/shrimp. Serve in crunchy iceberg lettuce cups and finish with the Nerigoma Dressing.

PINK PANCAKES WITH GOAT'S CHEESE, ONION RELISH & WALNUTS

PINK PANCAKE BATTER
2 eggs
220 ml/scant 1 cup whole milk
100 g/³/₄ cup plus 1 tablespoon plain/ all-purpose flour
pinch of salt
55 g/2 oz. cooked beetroot/ beet, finely chopped
1 tablespoon olive oil, plus extra for frying

FILLING
300 g/10½ oz. frozen spinach, thawed
300 g/10½ oz. soft goat's cheese
2 tablespoons freshly chopped basil
50 g/⅓ cup chopped walnuts
6 tablespoons grated vegetarian Parmesan cheese

ONION RELISH
2 tablespoons olive oil
3 onions, thinly sliced
2 tablespoons balsamic vinegar
2 tablespoons soft brown sugar
salt and freshly ground black pepper

TO SERVE
rocket/arugula
fresh basil leaves
vegetarian Parmesan shavings

MAKES 16 PANCAKES

The beetroot/beet adds colour to these pancakes, as well as a hint of earthy flavour, and the sour-sweet onion relish lifts the whole dish.

To make the onion relish, heat the olive oil in a saucepan over a low-medium heat. Add the onions, season and cook for 20 minutes, stirring occasionally, until soft and golden. Add the vinegar and sugar and cook for a further 5–10 minutes until jammy in consistency. Leave to cool.

To make the pancakes, place the eggs, half the milk, the flour, salt and chopped beetroot/beet in a food processor and blend until smooth. Add the remaining milk and the oil and blend again. Transfer to a jug/pitcher and leave to rest for 20 minutes.

To make the filling. Squeeze the excess water from the thawed spinach and chop finely. Place in a bowl and beat in the goat's cheese, basil, walnuts and grated vegetarian Parmesan. Season to taste with salt and pepper.

Lightly stir the pancake mixture once. Heat a frying pan/skillet over a medium heat, brush with oil and swirl in about 60 ml/¼ cup of the pancake mixture, making sure it covers the base. Cook over a medium-low heat for about 1½ minutes until the base is golden. Flip the pancake over and cook for a further 1 minute until dotted brown. Remove the pancake from the pan as soon as it is ready and keep warm while you cook the remaining batter in the same way.

When you are ready to serve, spoon the goat's cheese mixture down the centre of each pancake. Top with a few rocket/arugula leaves, fresh basil leaves and a spoonful of the onion relish. Roll up and serve with extra relish and shavings of vegetarian Parmesan cheese.

VE VEGAN CREPES WITH CREAMY SPINACH & BEETROOT FILLING
Make the Onion Relish as main recipe. Replace the Pink Pancakes with a dairy-free and egg-free recipe as follows (reallocating the beetroot/beet to the filling): Combine 165 ml/³/₄ cup soy milk and 110 ml/⅓ cup plus 2 tablespoons water in a mixing bowl. Add ¼ teaspoon bicarbonate of soda/baking soda and ¼ teaspoon salt. Slowly add 130 g/1 cup plain/all-purpose flour, whisking vigorously with a balloon whisk. Let rest for 15 minutes. Cook the pancakes as main recipe and keep warm. When filling, replace the goat's cheese with a soft vegan cheese (such as Violife) and the Parmesan with 4 tablespoons of Vegan Parmesan (see page 8). Stir the beetroot/beet into the filling. Finish as main recipe but with a dusting of Vegan Parmesan.

CAULIFLOWER-STUFED PACOS
WITH TAHINI & LIME YOGURT

PACO BATTER
225 g/1 cup ricotta cheese
3 tablespoons finely grated
  vegetarian Parmesan
  cheese
250 ml/1 cup plus
  1 tablespoon whole milk
1 tablespoon olive oil,
  plus extra for frying
2 UK large/US extra-large
  eggs, separated
150 g/1 cup plus
  2 tablespoons plain/
  all-purpose flour
1½ teaspoons baking
  powder

FILLING
350 g/4½ cups cauliflower
  florets
400-g/14-oz. can chickpeas
grated zest and freshly
  squeezed juice of 1 lime
1 teaspoon ras el hanout
1 tablespoon olive oil
½ red onion, thinly sliced
½ teaspoon white sugar
2 teaspoons white wine
  vinegar
100 g/generous ½ cup
  Greek yogurt
1 tablespoon tahini
salt and freshly ground
  black pepper
pomegranate seeds,
  to serve
handful of fresh coriander/
  cilantro leaves, to serve

*roasting pan, lined with
  baking parchment*

MAKES 6

Tacos lovers, meet your new best friend the 'paco', where a palm-sized pancake provides a perfect wrap for a Moroccan-inspired filling.

Preheat the oven to 190°C (375°F) Gas 5.

For the filling, cut any large cauliflower florets into bite-sized pieces and place in the prepared pan. Drain and rinse the chickpeas, then shake dry and add to the pan. Combine the lime zest, ras el hanout, olive oil and a little salt and pepper in a small bowl and stir well. Add this spice paste along with 1 tablespoon of water to the cauliflower mixture and stir to coat the ingredients evenly. Roast in the preheated oven for 20 minutes until the cauliflower is tender. After this, stir in 1 tablespoon lime juice and then turn the oven to its lowest setting to keep the filling warm.

Meanwhile, mix the red onion slices with the sugar, ½ teaspoon salt and the vinegar and set aside for 20 minutes. Drain well and then set aside. Combine the yogurt with the tahini and remaining lime juice and season with salt and pepper. Set aside until needed.

To make the pacos, place the ricotta, vegetarian Parmesan, milk, oil and egg yolks in a bowl and whisk well, then gradually whisk in the flour and baking powder with some salt and pepper. In a separate bowl, whisk the egg whites until just stiff, then fold through the batter until evenly combined.

When you are ready to serve, heat a pancake pan over a medium heat and brush with oil. Pour in about 250 ml/1 cup of the batter, allowing it to spread to about 14 cm/5½ inches across. Cook for about 2 minutes until golden and then flip and cook for a further 1 minute or so until evenly golden on both sides. Remove the pancake from the pan as soon as it's ready and keep warm while you cook the remaining batter in the same way, brushing the pan with oil as needed.

To serve, combine the cauliflower mixture with the pickled red onion, pomegranate seeds and coriander/cilantro in a bowl. Divide between the pancakes and drizzle over the yogurt tahini sauce.

VE SOCCA WITH SPICY CAULIFLOWER & CHICKPEAS Substitute a coconut yogurt or soy cream in place of the Greek yogurt when preparing the tahini and lime dressing. Replace the pacos with Socca Pancakes (see page 28) and serve as main recipe.

MUSHROOM BURGERS ⓥ

Creamy Camembert cheese pairs well with mushrooms in this satisfying
and tasty vegetarian take on a classic hamburger with all the trimmings.

2 tablespoons olive oil
1 large red onion, halved
 and thinly sliced
2 fresh thyme sprigs
¼ teaspoon white sugar
1 teaspoon balsamic
 vinegar
2 teaspoons butter
2 very large, flat
 mushrooms, stalks
 removed
salt and freshly ground
 black pepper

TO SERVE
burger buns, halved
mayonnaise
iceberg lettuce
thin slices of Camembert

SERVES 2

Heat 1 tablespoon of the olive oil in a large, heavy frying pan/skillet.
Add the red onion and thyme and fry gently over a low heat for
8 minutes, stirring now and then, until softened. Add the sugar and
vinegar and fry for 2 minutes more until caramelized. Set aside.

Wipe the frying pan/skillet clean. Heat the remaining 1 tablespoon
olive oil and butter over a medium heat. Add the mushrooms and fry
for 5 minutes, turning often, until browned on both sides. Season with
salt and freshly ground black pepper.

Briefly grill/broil the burger buns, cut-side up, until just golden.
Spread the bottom half with mayonnaise. Layer lettuce, a mushroom,
Camembert cheese and half the caramelized onions in each bun.
Serve at once.

ⓋⒺ **MUSHROOM BURGER WITH VEGAN CHEESE & CARAMELIZED ONION**
Omit the butter when frying the mushroom, using a little extra oil if necessary. Replace the
mayonnaise with a ready-made vegan mayo (such as Hellmann's) and add slices of Vegan
Cheese (see page 8) or your favourite store-bought vegan cheese in place of the Camembert
(try Mouse's Favourite Camembert-style Cashew Cheese). Add a few slices of fresh tomato
on top of the lettuce for umami and extra zing.

TENDERSTEM BROCCOLI, SHIITAKE & TOFU OMELETTE Ⓥ

This omelette/omelet has a distinctly Asian feel with creamy cubes of tofu replacing the more traditional cheese. This is perfect for a light, midweek supper.

1 tablespoon light olive oil
2 shallots, sliced
1 bunch of tenderstem broccoli, chopped into small pieces
200 g/7 oz. shiitake mushrooms
handful of baby spinach leaves, washed and stems removed
2 teaspoons light soy sauce or tamari, as preferred, plus extra to serve
300 g/10½ oz. firm tofu, cubed
8 eggs, lightly beaten
ground white pepper

SERVES 4

Put the oil in a large, non-stick frying pan/skillet and set over high heat. Add the shallots, broccoli and mushrooms and stir-fry for 3–4 minutes, until the mushrooms are soft and the broccoli turns a bright, emerald green. Add the spinach and cook until just wilted. Add the soy sauce and stir. Arrange the cubes of tofu over the vegetables so that they are evenly spaced. Preheat the grill/broiler to high.

Pour the beaten eggs into the pan and cook over high heat until the edges have puffed up.

Keep the omelette in the pan, place it under the preheated grill and cook until golden and firm on top.

Remove and let cool, then sprinkle with ground white pepper and drizzle with a little soy or tamari, if liked, to serve.

PE CHINESE BROCCOLI, PRAWN/SHRIMP & TOFU OMELETTE Take inspiration from the classic Chinese dish Prawns & Tofu Over Broccoli. Omit the shitake, halve the quantity of tofu and add with 100 g/3½ oz. of cooked, peeled prawns/shrimp. Add these with the tofu and finish as the main recipe. Serve drizzled with oyster sauce, if liked.

FENNEL, WATERCRESS & RED ONION GRATIN WITH THYME v

Fennel can be intense in flavour, so boil it for a while and what remains is delicious and well balanced when paired with sweet red onions and watercress.

2 fennel bulbs, thinly sliced

4 large red onions, thinly sliced

leaves of a bunch of fresh thyme

100 g/2 cups watercress leaves

500 ml/2 cups double/ heavy cream

3 slices of bread

50 g/²⁄₃ cup grated vegetarian Parmesan cheese

salt

SERVES 4

Preheat the oven to 160°C (325°F) Gas 3.

Put the fennel in a saucepan, cover with water, add a little salt and bring to a simmer over a medium heat. Continue to simmer for 10 minutes, then drain.

Add the red onions, thyme and watercress to the pan of boiled fennel and mix together. Spoon the greens into four individual ovenproof dishes, just cover with cream and a light sprinkling of salt.

Bake in the preheated oven for 20 minutes.

Put the bread, cheese and a generous pinch of salt into a food processor and blitz to a fine crumb.

Remove the dishes from the oven and sprinkle with the breadcrumbs.

Increase the oven to 180°C (350°F) Gas 4 and return the dishes to the oven for a further 10 minutes, until the tops are golden.

Serve warm from the oven, seasoned with a little salt.

VE FENNEL & TOMATO GRATIN WITH BLACK OLIVE CRUMB
Replace the thyme with a pinch of dried mixed herbs, omit the watercress and add 1 large ripe tomato to keep things moist. Slice the tomato and lay it on top of the fennel and red onion mixture in the baking dish. Replace the cream with 350 ml/1½ cups of Vegan Cream (see page 8) or any dairy-free cream. Omit the Parmesan and add 1 tablespoon of finely grated lemon zest and 5–6 pitted black olives to the breadcrumb mixture before blitzing. Season the mixture well with black pepper, sprinkle it over the gratin and drizzle the whole dish with a little olive oil before returning to the oven to finish as the main recipe.

HALLOUMI & VEGETABLE KEBABS WITH BAY LEAVES ⬣ V

Pleasingly plump button mushrooms, salty halloumi cheese and juicy cherry tomatoes combine well here, offering a taste of the Mediterranean. Cook over a barbecue/outdoor grill for extra flavour but if not available, your grill/broiler will do just as well. Serve with a peppery rocket/arugula and red onion salad on the side, if liked.

250 g/9 oz. halloumi cheese, cut into 16 even-sized pieces
16 button mushrooms, stalks trimmed off
12 cherry tomatoes
2 tablespoons olive oil
1 tablespoon freshly chopped flat-leaf parsley
8 fresh bay leaves, stalks trimmed, halved
8 thin lemon slices
salt and freshly ground black pepper

DRESSING
2 tablespoons extra virgin olive oil
1 tablespoon freshly squeezed lemon juice
1 tablespoon finely chopped flat-leaf parsley leaves
small pinch of sugar
salt and freshly ground black pepper

8 metal cooking skewers

SERVES 4

Preheat the grill/broiler and line a grill/broiler pan with foil to catch any juices.

In a large bowl, toss together the halloumi cheese, button mushrooms, cherry tomatoes, olive oil and chopped parsley. Season with a little salt and freshly ground black pepper. Thread the cheese, mushrooms, cherry tomatoes, bay leaves and lemon slices onto the 8 skewers.

Grill/broil the halloumi skewers for 5 minutes, turning over halfway through, until the halloumi is golden-brown. Whisk the dressing ingredients together and drizzle over the kebabs/kabobs to serve.

PE **GREEK-STYLE SWORDFISH KEBABS** Replace the halloumi with 300 g/10 oz. of fresh swordfish steak cut into even-sized cubes. Add the finely grated zest of half a lemon to the bowl when combining the ingredients. Cook the skewers for 7–8 minutes to ensure the fish is slightly charred on the outside and cooked through. Omit the dressing and instead serve the kebabs/kabobs with store-bought or homemade tzatziki on the side.

VE **SMOKY TOFU & MUSHROOM KEBABS** Replace the halloumi with 225 g/8 oz. extra-firm smoked tofu, cut into even-sized cubes, and use as per the main recipe. Add a finely chopped fresh red chilli/chile (deseeded) to the dressing to add a little spicy heat, if liked.

SALADS
& SIDES

MELON, TOMATO & FETA SALAD

Perfect food for hot-weather dining. Sweet melon combined with juicy tomatoes and contrasted with salty feta, makes this a lovely refreshing dish. Serve with crusty bread to mop up every last drop of deliciousness.

1 cantaloupe melon, peeled, deseeded and diced
300 g/10 oz. ripe tomatoes, sliced into wedges
2 tablespoons extra virgin olive oil
1 tablespoon Sherry vinegar
2 tablespoons finely snipped fresh chives
100 g/3½ oz. feta cheese, diced
freshly ground black pepper

SERVES 4

Toss together all the melon and tomato pieces with the oil, vinegar and chives in a serving dish. Season well with pepper.

Gently mix in the diced feta cheese, being careful not to overmix and break up the cheese. Serve at once.

M **TOMATO, MELON, BLUE CHEESE & PARMA HAM SALAD** For a saltier contrast and a meat option, substitute the feta with chunks of a firm, crumbly blue cheese (such as Roquefort) and add about 100 g/3 oz. shredded Parma ham to the finished dish.

HAZELNUT, MUSHROOM & BULGUR WHEAT SALAD VE

Here raw mushrooms are combined to great effect with dry-fried hazelnuts, juicy tomatoes, bulgur wheat and a tangy pomegranate molasses dressing to make a vibrant, colourful salad, inspired by the flavours of the Middle East.

100 g/½ cup bulgur wheat
100 g/⅔ cup blanched
  hazelnuts
100 g/¾ cup cherry
  tomatoes, quartered
½ red (bell) pepper,
  deseeded and diced
1 spring onion/scallion,
  finely chopped
3 tablespoons extra virgin
  olive oil
3 tablespoons pomegranate
  molasses
50 g/1 small bunch
  fresh flat-leaf parsley,
  very finely chopped
150 g/5 oz. white/cup
  mushrooms, cleaned
  and thinly sliced
salt and freshly ground
  black pepper

SERVES 4

Soak the bulgur wheat in boiling water for 5 minutes to soften; drain.

Dry-fry the hazelnuts in a frying pan/skillet for 2–3 minutes until golden-brown, stirring often. Leave to cool and then finely chop.

In a large bowl, mix together the bulgur wheat, toasted hazelnuts, cherry tomatoes, red (bell) pepper and spring onion/scallion. Add the extra virgin olive oil and pomegranate molasses. Season well with salt and freshly ground black pepper, and mix thoroughly. Mix in the parsley, then the mushrooms. Serve at once.

V WARM HALLOUMI & BULGUR SALAD WITH POMEGRANATE SEEDS

Make the salad as main recipe, adding a handful of fresh pomegranate seeds. Slice a block of halloumi widthways into 8 slices, each about 1 cm/½ inch thick. Dust in a little seasoned plain/all-purpose flour. Heat 2 tablespoons of olive oil in a frying pan/skillet, add the cheese slices (in batches if necessary) and fry, turning once, until golden on both sides. Serve 2 slices of warm halloumi on top of each serving of the salad, drizzed with extra pomegranate molasses.

M BUTTERFLIED CHICKEN WITH BULGUR SALAD & WALNUTS

Lay 4 chicken breasts on a cutting board, place your hand on top and carefully slice through each one lengthways. Heat 1 tablespoon of vegetable oil in a frying pan/skillet over a medium heat. Season the butterflied chicken breast with salt. Place it in the pan and cook for about 3 minutes on each side until golden brown. Check the chicken is cooked through: it should be firm to the touch and hot in the middle. Rest for 2–3 minutes before serving. When making the salad substitute walnuts for the hazelnuts and fresh coriander/cilantro for the flat-leaf parsley. Serve the chicken hot, drizzled with extra pomegranate molasses.

MUSHROOM, CANNELLINI BEAN & TUNA SALAD PE

The simple flavours of tuna fish and beans are given a savoury kick by a zingy anchovy, mustard and lemon juice dressing. Serve for a light lunch or supper, with toasted rustic bread on the side.

2 anchovy fillets
1 garlic clove, peeled
    and chopped
12 g/2 sprigs of fresh
    flat-leaf parsley
6 tablespoons olive oil,
    plus extra for serving
1 teaspoon Dijon mustard
grated zest and freshly
    squeezed juice of
    1 lemon
2 x 400-g/14-oz. cans
    of cannellini beans in
    water, drained and rinsed
150 g/5 oz. white/cup
    mushrooms, thinly sliced
150 g/5 oz. canned tuna
    in olive oil, drained
1 tablespoon finely chopped
    red onion or shallot
freshly ground
    black pepper

SERVES 4

First, make a dressing by blitzing together the anchovy fillets, garlic, parsley (reserving a little to garnish), olive oil, mustard and lemon juice in a food processor until smooth.

Toss the cooked cannellini beans with the dressing and place in a serving dish.

Fold in two-thirds of the sliced mushrooms. Top with chunks of tuna and the remaining mushroom slices. Drizzle with a little olive oil, sprinkle with the reserved chopped parsley, red onion and lemon zest. Season with freshly ground black pepper and serve.

VE **SUN-DRIED TOMATO & CANNELLINI BEAN SALAD WITH CAPER & LEMON DRESSING** Omit the tuna from the recipe and replace with about 100 g/3½ oz. chopped sun-dried tomatoes. Replace the anchovy fillets in the dressing with 2 tablespoons of drained capers and prepare as the main recipe. Season well and serve the salad on a bed of peppery rocket/arugula.

SMOKED TROUT FATTOUSH
WITH SUMAC PE

Fattoush is a fresh-tasting salad from the Lebanon. Despite its exotic name, the ingredients are basically summer garden produce – cucumber, tomato, parsley and mint – with the addition of crisp pieces of toasted bread, but without these pieces of bread it just isn't fattoush!

2 pitta breads, white or
   wholemeal as preferred
125 ml/½ cup olive oil
2 smoked trout fillets
1 small head of cos/
   Romaine lettuce,
   shredded
1 large cucumber,
   cut into thin batons
4 Roma tomatoes,
   halved and sliced
1 small red onion,
   thinly sliced
large handful of freshly
   chopped flat-leaf parsley
handful of freshly chopped
   mint
3 tablespoons freshly
   squeezed lemon juice
2 teaspoons ground sumac

SERVES 4

Preheat the oven to 180°C (350°F) Gas 4.

Split the pitta breads in half and brush lightly with some of the olive oil. Put on a baking sheet and cook in the preheated oven for about 10 minutes, turning after 5 minutes, until golden. While still warm, break the bread into smaller pieces and set aside on a wire rack to cool and crisp up.

Carefully pull the skin off the trout and discard. Gently fork the flesh from the bones and flake into smaller pieces.

Put the lettuce, cucumber, tomato, onion and herbs in a large salad bowl. Add the trout and pitta bread pieces and gently toss to combine without breaking up the trout too much.

Put the remaining olive oil in a small bowl. Add the lemon juice and whisk with a fork until emulsified. Pour the dressing over the salad and sprinkle with sumac, if using. Serve immediately.

V GREEK SALAD FATTOUSH Omit the trout and add a 200 g/7 oz. cubed feta cheese and a handful of pitted oven-dried black olives.

VE FATTOUSH WITH CHICKPEAS & BEETROOT Omit the smoked trout and replace with a 400-g/14-oz. can drained and rinsed chickpeas. Add 100 g/3½ oz. of the Salt-baked Beetroot (see page 32) or diced cooked beetroot/beet, as preferred.

CHARRED CAESAR SALAD
WITH GARLIC CROUTONS Ⓥ

This salad was invented by chef Caesar Cardini (of Italian descent) in Tijuana, Mexico, for American tourists. A lot of recipes for a Caesar salad add anchovies to the dressing, but this can detract from the flavours of garlic and fresh, charred lettuce that work so well together here, and leaving them out creates a vegetarian version.

200 ml/¾ cup extra virgin olive oil, plus extra to drizzle
2 garlic cloves, crushed
4 slices sourdough bread, cut into 1-cm/⅜-inch cubes
2 heads of cos/romaine lettuce, halved lengthways
freshly squeezed juice of ½ lemon
1 egg yolk
100 g/3½ oz. vegetarian Parmesan cheese
vegetarian Worcester sauce (such as Biona or Geo Organics), to drizzle (optional)

SERVES 4

Firstly, you need to make garlic oil. Heat the oil and crushed garlic cloves in a pan but do not let them burn, then leave to cool for at least an hour, while the flavours infuse.

Preheat the oven to 180°C (350°F) Gas 4.

Toss the sourdough cubes in the garlic oil until evenly coated. Spread out on a baking sheet and cook in the preheated oven for 20 minutes or until golden. Once removed from the oven, they will continue to crisp up even more as they cool.

Drizzle a little of the oil over the cut surface of the lettuce heads. Preheat a griddle/ridged grill pan over a high heat and place the lettuce cut-side down in the pan. Cook for a few minutes until just starting to blacken.

Make the salad dressing by putting the garlic oil, lemon juice and egg yolk in a screw-top jar, tightening the lid and shaking to combine.

To serve, arrange the lettuce halves, cut-side up, on plates. Finely grate half of the vegetarian Parmesan over the top – it should begin to melt. Sprinkle the croutons over the plate.

Dress the salad with the salad dressing, then drizzle with a little vegetarian Worcester sauce (if using) and shave the remaining Parmesan over the top before serving.

PE PAN-FRIED SALMON CAESAR SALAD Prepare the garlic croutons and lettuce as main recipe. Allow 1 x 250-g/9-oz. boneless salmon fillet per serving. Heat 1 tablespoon of vegetable oil in a large frying pan/skillet. Season the salmon with black pepper and fry/sauté for 2–3 minutes on each side. Remove the skin from the fish and flake the fillets over the prepared salad. Drizzle with the Caesar dressing to serve (omit the Worcester sauce).

CHICKPEA & MUSHROOM FREEKEH PILAF VE

With its subtle smoky flavour, freekeh (made from young durum wheat) is a great grain to cook with. Here, it is combined with nutty chickpeas and earthy mushrooms to make an appealing, colourful Middle Eastern-style pilaf.

1 tablespoon olive oil
1 red onion, ½ chopped, ½ sliced
½ cinnamon stick
3 cardamom pods
½ tablespoon coriander seeds
250 g/1¼ cups freekeh (roasted green durum wheat), rinsed
400 ml/1⅔ cups vegetable stock
1 tablespoon olive oil
1 garlic clove, chopped
250 g/9 oz. white/cup mushrooms, sliced 1 cm/⅜ inch thick
400-g/14-oz. can of chickpeas in water, drained
salt
4 tablespoons pomegranate seeds, to garnish
freshly chopped coriander/cilantro, to garnish

SERVES 4

Heat the oil in a heavy-based saucepan. Add the chopped red onion, cinnamon stick, cardamom and coriander seeds and fry, stirring a little, over a gentle heat for 2–3 minutes.

Add the freekeh, mixing well to coat in the flavoured oil. Add the stock and season with salt. Bring to the boil. Cover, reduce the heat and simmer for 20–25 minutes over a very low heat until the stock has reduced and the freekeh grains have softened.

Heat the olive oil in a frying pan/skillet. Fry the sliced red onion and garlic over a medium heat for 2 minutes, until softened and fragrant. Add the mushrooms and fry over a high heat, stirring, until lightly browned.

Fold two-thirds of the chickpeas into the freekeh. Place the mixture in a serving dish. Top with the freshly fried mushrooms and remaining chickpeas. Sprinkle with the pomegranate seeds and coriander/cilantro to garnish. Serve at once.

M GRIDDLED LAMB CUTLETS WITH FREEKAH PILAF & YOGURT
Season 4 lamb cutlets with salt and pepper. Heat a griddle/ridged grill pan and when it is hot, cook the lamb, turning occasionally for 7–8 minutes. Remove from the pan, cover with foil and leave to rest for 2 minutes. Serve the pilaf as an accompaniment to the cutlets, with plain/natural yogurt on the side for spooning, dusted with a little smoked paprika, if liked.

TABBOULEH VE

This zingy tomato and parsley salad is a mezze classic, traditionally served as a small dish, it goes well with the Halloumi & Vegetable Kebabs on page 44.

1 tablespoon bulgur wheat
350 g/12 oz. ripe but firm
   tomatoes
100 g/1 cup fresh
   flat-leaf parsley
1 spring onion/scallion,
   finely chopped
2 tablespoons finely sliced
   mint leaves
freshly squeezed juice
   of 1 lemon
2 tablespoons extra virgin
   olive oil
salt and freshly ground
   black pepper
fresh mint sprigs,
   to garnish

SERVES 4

Soak the bulgur wheat in cold water for 15 minutes to soften.

Meanwhile, finely dice the tomatoes, discarding the white stem base. Trim off and discard the stalks of the flat-leaf parsley and finely chop the leaves. If using a food processor, take care not to over-chop the parsley as it may turn to a pulp; you want the parsley to retain its texture.

Drain the soaked bulgur wheat, squeezing it dry of excess moisture. Toss together the diced tomatoes, chopped parsley, bulgur wheat, spring onion/scallion and mint. Add the lemon juice, oil, season with salt and pepper, and toss well.

Garnish the tabbouleh with mint and serve at once.

PE **MOROCCAN SEABASS WITH HERBY TABBOULEH** Take 4 boneless seabass fillets. Put 4 tablespoons harissa paste, the zest and juice of 1 lemon, 1 crushed garlic clove, ½ teaspoon ground cumin, a pinch each of ground cinnamon and nutmeg and 2 tablespoons of olive oil in a bowl and mix. Rub this paste all over the fish fillets and lay them skin-side down on a large baking sheet lined with baking parchment. Bake in an oven preheated to 180°C (350°F) Gas 4 for 12–15 minutes. Meanwhile prepare the tabbouleh, replacing the mint with finely chopped fresh coriander/cilantro. Serve each fillet plated with the tabbouleh on the side.

KACHUMBER VE

Piquant green chilli/chile, fragrant cumin, tangy lemon juice and fresh mint combine to give a vibrant kick to this classic, easy-to-make, appealingly textured Indian salad. Serve it as an accompaniment to dishes such as tandoori prawns/shrimp (see below), or a pan-fried salmon fillet (see page 101).

600 g/1¼ lbs. ripe tomatoes
1 shallot
½ cucumber
2 teaspoons cumin seeds
1 green chilli/chile,
    deseeded and finely
    chopped
handful of freshly shredded
    mint leaves
freshly squeezed juice
    of ¼ lemon
salt and freshly ground
    black pepper
4 lemon wedges, to serve

SERVES 4

Begin by scalding the tomatoes. Pour boiling water over the ripe tomatoes in a heatproof bowl. Set aside for 1 minute, then drain and carefully peel off the skins using a sharp knife. Slice the tomatoes in half, scoop out and remove the pulp and slice the tomato shells.

Peel the shallot, slice lengthways and finely slice into semi-circles. Put the shallot slices in a colander and pour over freshly boiled water. Pat dry with paper towels and set aside.

Peel the cucumber, slice in half lengthways and scoop out the seeds. Finely slice and set aside.

Toast the cumin seeds in a small, dry, heavy-bottomed frying pan/skillet until fragrant. Swirl the pan regularly so that they don't burn. Remove from the pan and set aside to cool.

Toss together the chopped tomatoes, shallot, cucumber, green chilli/chile and toasted cumin seeds. Season with salt and pepper, add the mint leaves and lemon juice and toss to combine.

Serve at once with a wedge of lemon on the side of each portion.

PE **TANDOORI PRAWNS/SHRIMP WITH KACHUMBER** Mix 1 tablespoon tandoori curry powder, 2 tablespoons sunflower oil, 1 tablespoon natural/plain yogurt and the zest and juice of 1 lime in a large bowl. Add 170 g/6 oz. cooked king prawns/jumbo shrimp and toss to coat. Preheat the grill/broiler to high. Skewer the prawns/shrimp onto 3–4 metal skewers and cook under the grill/broiler for 2 minutes on each side, until golden. Serve with the kachumber on the side and an extra dollop of the yogurt mixed with a pinch of dried mint.

SOUPS
& STEWS

VEGETABLE MINESTRONE

2 tablespoons olive oil
1 large onion, diced
3 carrots, peeled and diced
1 celery stick/rib, sliced
1 leek, sliced
3 potatoes, peeled and diced
2 garlic cloves, crushed
400-g/14-oz. can chopped
   tomatoes
1.5 litres/6 cups vegetable
   stock
handful (about 70 g/2½ oz.)
   of broken spaghetti,
   or similar
400-g/14-oz. can cannellini
   or haricot/navy beans,
   drained
250 g/9 oz. spinach or
   other greens, chopped
1–2 courgettes/zucchini,
   diced
bunch of fresh flat-leaf
   parsley, chopped
1 teaspoon mixed
   dried herbs
paprika, to taste (optional)
salt and freshly ground
   black pepper
vegetarian Parmesan
   (optional)

SERVES 6

Having a good minestrone recipe up your sleeve can be a life saver as it's a great way to use up leftovers of vegetables that lurk in the fridge. Adapt this recipe as you see fit, and use any veggies you like to create your own favourite. For a vegan option, simply replace the vegetarian Parmesan with a sprinkle of the Vegan Parmesan on page 8.

Heat the olive oil in a large saucepan and add the onion, carrots, celery, leek and potatoes, put the lid on the pan and sweat for a few minutes over a gentle heat, until the vegetables soften without colouring. Add the garlic to the pan and continue cooking for a few minutes before adding the chopped tomatoes, stock and pasta. Bring the liquid to the boil, then reduce to a simmer and cook until the vegetables are just tender and the pasta is almost cooked. Add the beans, greens, courgettes/zucchini and parsley to the pan and continue to cook for a few minutes until the greens are tender but still green. Season to taste with salt and pepper and, if you like a little heat, stir in a little paprika.

Serve generous portions of the soup in bowls and finish with plenty of freshly grated vegetarian Parmesan.

Ⓜ CLASSIC MINESTRONE Increase the quantity of olive oil to 2 tablespoons and heat it in a large saucepan. Chop 2 rashers/slices bacon and sauté until browned, before adding the onion, carrots, celery, leek and potatoes. Finish as the main recipe, and top with a generous amount of finely grated regular Parmesan.

CREAMY CELERIAC & WHITE BEAN SOUP WITH HAZELNUTS ⓥ

Celeriac has such a wonderful nutty sweetness. The starch from the smooth white beans gives this soup a luxurious richness, while the hazelnuts and truffle oil add extra texture and flavour. This is definitely an impressive soup for entertaining.

150 g/1 cup hazelnuts
90 ml/6 tablespoons
   olive oil
8 banana shallots,
   finely diced
2 garlic cloves,
   roughly chopped
2 celeriac/celery root,
   peeled and diced
2 celery sticks/ribs, sliced
2 bay leaves
2 litres/quarts vegetable
   stock
400-g/14-oz. can cannellini
   beans, drained
180 ml/¾ cup double/
   heavy cream
freshly squeezed lemon
   juice, to taste
sea salt and freshly ground
   black pepper
hazelnut oil or truffle oil,
   to serve (optional)

SERVES 6–8

Preheat the oven to 190°C (375°F) Gas 5.

Put the hazelnuts in a roasting pan and into the preheated oven for about 10 minutes, until they are just golden and fragrant. Tip the toasted nuts into a tea/dish towel and rub well to remove the skins, then roughly chop them.

Put the olive oil, shallots, garlic, celeriac/celery root, celery and bay leaves in a saucepan and toss over medium–high heat for a few minutes, until beginning to soften. Add the stock to the pan along with three-quarters of the toasted hazelnuts and the cannellini beans. Cover the pan and simmer gently for about 15–20 minutes, until the celeriac/celery root is very tender.

Draw the pan off the heat and remove the bay leaves.

With a stick blender, whizz the soup until very smooth, then stir in the cream and blend briefly again until well mixed. If the soup is a little thin, allow to simmer gently over a very low heat to reduce down a little – this should be a smooth, velvety soup. When you are happy with the consistency, season with salt and pepper and a squeeze of lemon juice.

Ladle the soup into bowls, scatter the remaining toasted hazelnuts over the top and drizzle with hazelnut or truffle oil to serve.

Ⓜ **CREAMED CELERIAC & CHICKEN SOUP** Cover 2 bone-in chicken breasts (with the skin on) in 2 litres/quarts cold water. Add 2 teaspoons of vegetable bouillon powder, a pinch of dried mixed herbs and season with salt and pepper. Bring to a boil over a high heat and, once the liquid is boiling, skim the foam from the surface and reduce the heat to a simmer. Cook for about 30 minutes, until the chicken is cooked through. Strain the cooking water through a fine sieve/strainer and discard the seasonings. Use this cooking liquid in place of the vegetable stock in the main recipe. Use your fingers to shred the chicken and add this to the finished soup, reheating as necessary to warm the chicken through. Finish as the main recipe.

VELVETY PUMPKIN & RED LENTIL SOUP VE

This golden and beautifully seasoned vegan soup is the perfect comforting one-bowl meal for autumn/fall, rich with lentils and winter squash, it is very filling.

70 g/½ cup chopped leek (white part) or onion
4 tablespoons olive oil
200 g/1⅔ cups peeled and seeded pumpkin wedges cut into 3–4-cm/1¼–1½-inch chunks
120 g/1 cup carrot cut into 2.5-cm/1-inch pieces
1 teaspoon vegetable bouillon powder
¼ teaspoon ground turmeric
4 garlic cloves, crushed
2 bay leaves
3 dried tomato halves, chopped
2 tablespoons vegan white wine
150 g/¾ cup dried red lentils, washed and drained
7-cm/2¾-inch strip of kombu seaweed
squeeze of lemon juice
1 tablespoon umeboshi vinegar
salt and freshly ground black pepper

SERVES 4

In a large saucepan, sauté the leek or onion in the olive oil with a pinch of salt, uncovered, until the vegetables are soft and transparent.

Add the pumpkin and carrot and sauté until the vegetables start to 'sweat'. Add the bouillon powder, turmeric, garlic, bay leaves and tomatoes and stir. Next, pour in the wine and let the mixture boil.

Now it's time to add the lentils, kombu and 1 litre/4 cups water. Turn up the heat, cover and bring to the boil. Then, lower the heat and let simmer for about 25–30 minutes or until the lentils and vegetables are completely tender.

At this point, remove the bay leaves. Use a handheld blender to purée the soup and make it smooth and creamy.

Add lemon juice, a few grinds of black pepper and the umeboshi vinegar to taste and stir. You can add more hot water if the soup seems too thick, but it will definitely thicken as it cools.

Ladle into bowls to serve.

V BUTTERNUT, BEETROOT/BEET & RED LENTIL SOUP Prepare as main recipe but replace the pumpkin with butternut squash, half the olive oil with 2 tablespoons butter and omit the kombu. Add 80 g/⅔ cup of peeled and diced raw beetroot/beet with the squash and carrot, and finish as main recipe, adding a swirl of crème fraîche or sour cream.

M CHUNKY LENTIL & HAM HOCK SOUP Prepare as main recipe but leave the soup unblended so that it is chunky and more stew-like. Add 90 g/3 oz. ready-cooked pulled or shredded ham hock to the soup (available from larger supermarkets) before seasoning to taste. Reheat just to warm the ham through before serving.

TOFU & MUSHROOM HOTPOT VE

Mushrooms and tofu have an affinity as ingredients, and they are combined here in a fresh vegetarian take on a classic Chinese hotpot. Serve with steamed rice.

400 g/14 oz. firm tofu,
  well drained
8 dried shiitake mushrooms
1 tablespoon cornflour/
  cornstarch
2 tablespoons vegetable oil
½ onion, chopped
1 leek, finely sliced
2.5-cm/1-inch piece of root
  ginger, finely chopped
1 garlic clove, chopped
¼ head of Chinese leaf/
  napa cabbage, roughly
  chopped
3 tablespoons rice wine
  or Amontillado sherry
pinch of Chinese five spice
  powder
150 g/5 oz. assorted fresh
  mushrooms (oyster,
  shiitake, eryngii),
  large ones halved
1 tablespoon light soy sauce
pinch of sugar
1 teaspoon sesame seed oil
salt
chopped spring onion/
  scallion, to garnish
steamed rice, to serve

SERVES 4

Wrap the tofu in paper towels and place a weighty item (such as a heavy baking sheet) on top. Leave for at least 10 minutes to let the excess moisture drain.

Soak the dried shiitake mushrooms in 200 ml/1 scant cup of hot water for 20 minutes. Strain through a fine-mesh sieve/strainer, reserving the soaking liquid. Trim and discard the tough stalks from the shiitake and cut them in half.

Cut the tofu into cubes and roll them in the cornflour/cornstarch to coat. Heat 1 tablespoon of the oil in a frying pan/skillet. Fry the tofu for 5 minutes over a medium-high heat, turning over during frying, until lightly browned on all sides.

Heat the remaining oil in a casserole dish or Dutch oven over a medium heat. Add the onion, leek, ginger and garlic and fry, stirring, for 2 minutes. Add the Chinese leaf/napa cabbage and fry for a further 2 minutes. Mix in the rice wine or sherry and five spice powder and cook for 1 minute. Add the fried tofu, soaked shiitake and the fresh mushrooms.

Pour in the reserved shiitake soaking liquid, soy sauce and add the pinch of sugar. Bring to the boil. Cover and cook over a medium heat for 15 minutes. Uncover and cook for 10 minutes, stirring gently now and then. Season with salt. Stir in the sesame seed oil. Serve straight away, garnished with chopped spring onion/scallion.

M CHICKEN & TOFU HOTPOT WITH MUSHROOMS Reduce the quantity of tofu in the main recipe to 200 g/7 oz. Put 2 boneless and skinless chicken breasts in a saucepan and cover with cold water. Bring to a boil over a high heat and once the liquid is boiling, reduce the heat to a simmer. Cook, uncovered, for about 10–15 minutes, until the chicken is cooked through. Remove from the water with a slotted spoon, pat dry and shred. Add this shredded chicken to the hotpot 2 minutes before the end of cooking time to just to heat through.

BORLOTTI BEAN & FENNEL STEW VE

This delicious and comforting stew is inspired by the flavours of Sicily where fennel grows in abundance and is used in many traditional dishes. Serve with plenty of crusty bread to mop up the delicious red wine-infused sauce.

1 large or 2 small
  fennel bulbs
1 tablespoon olive oil
150 g/5 oz. small onion or
  large shallot, chopped
2 garlic cloves, crushed
400-g/14-oz. can chopped
  tomatoes
100 ml/1/3 cup vegan
  red wine
400-g/14-oz. can borlotti
  beans, drained and
  rinsed
1 teaspoon fennel seeds,
  crushed
2–3 fresh sage leaves
1 fresh or dried bay leaf
crusty bread, to serve

SERVES 2

Trim the fennel, making sure to keep any green feathery fronds for garnishing later. Cut it into wedges, leaving the base intact so that it holds the leaves together while they cook.

Heat the oil in a medium-sized frying pan/skillet, and gently brown the onion or shallot and fennel, then add crushed garlic cloves and cook for another 1–2 minutes.

Add the tomatoes, wine, beans, fennel seeds, sage and bay leaf. Cover the pan/skillet and cook gently for about 40 minutes.

Sprinkle with the reserved chopped fennel fronds and serve with crusty bread.

M **PORK SHOULDER & BORLOTTI BEAN STEW WITH FENNEL** Take 225 g/8 oz. of pork shoulder/Boston butt, cut it into 5-cm/2-inch cubes and rub these with the crushed fennel seeds before adding to the pan with the onion and fennel wedges. Fry/sauté until the meat is browned and then finish the stew as the main recipe. Check and add a little water halfway through the cooking time if necessary. Serve with mashed potatoes, if liked.

BEANS À LA BOURGUIGNONNE
WITH GARLIC & PARSLEY BUTTER ⓥ

This bean-based variation of the classic French beef stew (that was once staple bistro fare) makes a filling and nourishing vegetarian dish. A garlic and parsley butter is stirred in just before serving to add a final French flourish! Simply substitute the wine for a vegan wine and a non-dairy spread for a vegan option.

1 tablespoon olive oil
10 baby onions or shallots, peeled, but left whole
2 carrots, peeled and diced
1 garlic clove, crushed
250 g/9 oz. button mushrooms, cleaned
150 ml/²/₃ cup red wine
150 ml/²/₃ cup vegetable stock
1½ x 400-g/14-oz. cans red kidney beans, drained and rinsed
1 fresh or dried bay leaf
½ celery stick/rib, trimmed
1 fresh thyme sprig or 1 teaspoon dried thyme
salt and freshly ground black pepper
sugar, to taste (optional)

GARLIC & PARSLEY BUTTER
15 g/1 tablespoon butter, softened
1 garlic clove, finely chopped
leaves from a small bunch of fresh flat-leaf parsley, very finely chopped

SERVES 4

Heat the oil in a saucepan and fry the baby onions or shallots and the carrots until they begin to brown. Stir in the crushed garlic and continue to cook for 1–2 minutes, until the garlic no longer smells raw.

Add the mushrooms and fry them until tender and lightly browned, then pour in the red wine, bring to the boil and simmer for 5 minutes.

Add the stock and the beans with enough of their cooking water to cover. Add the bay leaf, celery and thyme, pushed down well so that they are covered with liquid. Cover tightly and simmer gently for 1 hour, until the beans are thoroughly cooked and and the flavours are blended. (This can be done on the hob/stovetop, or in an oven at 150°C (300°F) Gas 2 in an ovenproof casserole dish with a tight-fitting lid.) Check the seasoning and add salt and pepper to taste, plus a pinch of sugar if necessary to counteract the acidity of the wine.

Blend the softened butter with the chopped parsley leaves and the chopped garlic, and stir into the casserole dish just before serving.

Ⓜ **BEAN & SMOKED BACON BOURGUIGNONNE** Start the main recipe by frying/sautéing 100 g/3½ oz. smoked bacon lardons in a frying pan/skillet in 1 tablespoon of butter until brown. Remove the lardons from the pan and set aside. Prepare the dish following the main recipe and reintroduce the cooked bacon lardons to the pan with the stock and beans. Finish as main recipe.

SYRIAN AUBERGINE & CHICKPEA RAGOUT
WITH GARLIC YOGURT SAUCE Ⓥ

Roasted chunks of aubergine/eggplant and nutty chickpeas, bound together in a sweet tomato and onion sauce enriched with herbs and spices — this dish is popular in both Syria and Lebanon, where it is served with warm bread as part of a selection of mezze, or with rice as a main dish. Simply omit the traditional accompaniment of Garlic Yogurt Sauce or replace with a Garlicky Hummus dressing (see below) for a vegan option.

2 aubergines/eggplants
(about 500 g/1 lb in total)
4 tablespoons olive oil
1 large onion, finely sliced
4 garlic cloves, finely sliced
½ teaspoon each ground
cinnamon and freshly
grated nutmeg
generous bunch of flat-leaf
parsley, chopped
4 tomatoes, skinned
and chopped
400-g/14-oz. can chickpeas,
drained and rinsed
2 tablespoons freshly
chopped mint
salt and freshly ground
black pepper
freshly chopped coriander/
cilantro, to garnish

GARLIC YOGURT SAUCE
250 ml/1 cup Greek yogurt
1 teaspoon crushed garlic
½ teaspoon salt
1 tablespoon freshly
squeezed lemon juice

SERVES 6

Preheat the oven to 180°C (350°F) Gas 4.

Cut the aubergines/eggplants into 2-cm/¾-inch cubes, and toss in half of the olive oil, then spread out on a baking sheet and roast in the oven for about 20 minutes, turning the pieces over once halfway through cooking, until fairly soft. Set aside.

Meanwhile, in a saucepan over a gentle heat, soften the sliced onion and garlic in the remaining olive oil, adding a couple of tablespoons of water if necessary to prevent browning. This should take about 20 minutes, until the onion is golden and melting.

Add the spices and stir around for 1–2 minutes to blend the flavours, then tip in the parsley, chopped tomatoes and aubergine/eggplant, followed by the drained chickpeas. Add about 200 ml/scant 1 cup water, bring to the boil and then simmer, covered, for 20–30 minutes.

Take off the heat, stir in the fresh mint, adjust the seasoning and set aside for 1–2 hours before serving. In fact, the dish keeps perfectly well for a good 24 hours, and may even improve, and can be easily reheated.

Season with salt and pepper, sprinkle with the chopped coriander/cilantro and serve warm with a generous dollop of Garlic Yogurt Sauce.

VE AUBERGINE & CHICKPEA RAGOUT WITH GARLICKY HUMMUS Prepare the ragout as main recipe. Omit the Garlic Yogurt Sauce and serve instead with a dressing made by blending 80 g/⅓ cup prepared hummus with 2–3 chopped garlic cloves, ¼ teaspoon salt, 1 tablespoon olive oil, 1 tablespoon freshly squeezed lemon juice, ½ teaspoon ground turmeric and 60 ml/¼ Vegan Cream (see page 8) or any dairy-free cream. Drizzle over the dish to serve.

MUSHROOM & BEAN CHILI SIN CARNE Ⓥ

This vegetarian take on a classic chili con carne is simple and quick to make. Delicious served with crunchy tortilla chips or used to fill baked potatoes, it can be made a day in advance and kept in the fridge until needed. Simply substitute Vegan Cheese and Vegan Cream (see page 8) when serving for a vegan option.

1 tablespoon olive oil
1 onion, chopped
1 garlic clove, chopped
1 celery stalk, chopped
½ red (bell) pepper, finely chopped
150 g/5 oz. field mushrooms (Portabellini), finely chopped
1 teaspoon ground cumin
pinch of dried oregano
½ teaspoon smoked paprika
400-g/14-oz. can chopped tomatoes
1 teaspoon chipotle paste
pinch of sugar
400-g/14-oz. can kidney beans, drained and rinsed
200 g/7 oz. button mushrooms, halved if large
salt and freshly ground black pepper
freshly chopped coriander/cilantro, to garnish

TO SERVE (OPTIONAL)
sour cream
grated Cheddar cheese
tortilla chips

SERVES 4

Heat the oil over a medium heat in a casserole dish or Dutch oven. Add the onion, garlic, celery and red (bell) pepper and fry, stirring, for 5 minutes until softened. Add the field mushrooms (Portabellini), cumin, oregano and smoked paprika and fry, stirring, for 5 minutes.

Add the chopped tomatoes, 200 ml/1 scant cup of water, chipotle paste and sugar. Season with salt and pepper and stir well. Bring to the boil, then stir in the kidney beans and button mushrooms.

Lower the heat to medium and simmer, uncovered, for 15 minutes, stirring now and then. Portion into bowls and garnish with the chopped coriander/cilantro. Serve with sour cream, grated Cheddar cheese and tortilla chips, if liked.

Ⓜ **CHUNKY BEEF CHILI** Omit the red (bell) peppers and both types of mushroom and replace with 400 g/14 oz. diced stewing beef. Heat an additional 2 tablespoons of vegetable oil in a large saucepan. Add the cubed beef and cook for a few minutes on each side until browned all over. Remove from the pan with a slotted spoon and set aside. Follow the main recipe, reintroducing the beef to the pan with the chopped tomatoes, water, chipotle paste and sugar but hold back the kidney beans. Bring to a simmer, then cook, covered for about 1½–2 hours until the beef is tender. Add the kidney beans, stir and warm them through before serving.

WINTER VEGETABLE STEW
WITH HERBED DUMPLINGS

2 tablespoons olive oil
25 g/2 tablespoons butter
3 shallots, quartered
2 potatoes, cut into chunks
1 parsnip, cut into chunks
250 g/9 oz. baby carrots, whole
250 g/4 cups button mushrooms
1 leek, sliced into rings
2 garlic cloves, crushed
4 fresh thyme sprigs
1 teaspoon Dijon mustard
2 tablespoons plain/all-purpose flour
1 tablespoon balsamic vinegar
240 ml/1 cup white wine
400-g/14-oz. can butter/lima beans, drained and rinsed
250 g/9 oz. fresh raw beetroot/beets, peeled and cut into chunks
300 ml/1¼ cups vegetable stock
salt and freshly ground black pepper

HERBED DUMPLINGS
250 g (2 cups minus 1½ tablespoons) plain/all-purpose flour
2 teaspoons baking powder
125 g/1 stick plus 1 tablespoon butter, chilled
handful of any fresh green herbs
pinch of mustard powder
salt and freshly ground black pepper

SERVES 4

This stew is packed with root vegetables making it both hearty enough to satisfy on a cold winter's day but still a healthy choice.

Preheat the oven to 180°C (350°F) Gas 4.

Put the oil and butter in a flameproof casserole dish set over a medium-high heat. Add the shallots and cook for 2 minutes. Add the potatoes, parsnip, carrots, mushrooms and leek and cook for 5 minutes, stirring occasionally, until the vegetables start to turn golden. Turn the heat down slightly and add the garlic and thyme. Season generously with salt and pepper, then stir in the mustard. Add the flour and stir until the vegetables are well coated and the flour has disappeared. Add the vinegar and wine and cook for 2 minutes. Add the butter/lima beans and beetroot/beets, stir gently, then add the vegetable stock.

Bring the mixture to the boil and boil for 2 minutes. Then cover with a lid and transfer to the preheated oven. Bake for 40–50 minutes.

Meanwhile, prepare the dumplings. Sift the flour and baking powder into a bowl. Chop the cold butter into small pieces, then rub it into the flour. When it resembles breadcrumbs and there are no lumps of butter, stir in the chopped herbs and season with salt and pepper. Add a couple of tablespoons of water, or just enough to bring the mixture together to form a stiff dough.

Divide the dough into walnut-sized balls. Cover with clingfilm/plastic wrap and chill in the refrigerator until the stew is cooked. When the stew is ready, put the dumplings on the top of the stew so that they are half submerged. Cover with a lid and return the stew to the oven or put the casserole on the hob/stove over a low-medium heat, and cook for 20 minutes until the dumplings have puffed up and are golden on the top.

VE HEARTY VEGETABLE STEW WITH GARLIC & HERB TOASTS Prepare the stew as main recipe, replacing the butter with olive oil and the wine with vegan wine. Omit the Herbed Dumplings. Mix 2 tablespoons of vegan spread with 1 crushed garlic clove and 1 tablespoon of freshly chopped flat-leaf parsley. Spread on slices of toasted baguette and arrange on top of the stew to serve.

M SAUSAGE & ROOT VEGETABLE CASSEROLE Omit the Herbed Dumplings and prepare the stew as main recipe. Grill/broil or pan-fry 4 good-quality plain pork sausages until cooked through. Using metal tongs to grip them, use a sharp knife to slice them on the diagonal into quill shapes and stir these into the casserole whilst still hot and serve.

PUY LENTIL & SQUASH CASSEROLE WITH QUINOA VE

An earthy combination of flavours and textures makes this a satisfying vegan dish. Serve with nutty and nutritious quinoa for a hearty meal.

15 g/½ oz. assorted dried mushrooms (morels, porcini, girolles)
200 ml/scant 1 cup hot water
120 g/⅔ cup Puy/French green lentils
1 tablespoon olive oil
1 red onion, sliced
1 garlic clove, chopped
1 celery stick/rib, finely chopped
1 fresh rosemary sprig, leaves only
400-g/14-oz. can chopped tomatoes
pinch of sugar
400 g/14 oz. (1 small) butternut squash, peeled and cubed
200 g/7 oz. chestnut/cremini mushrooms, halved
salt and freshly ground black pepper
freshly chopped flat-leaf parsley, to garnish

SERVES 4

Soak the dried mushrooms in the hot water for 20 minutes. Strain, reserving the mushrooms and 100 ml/scant ½ cup of the soaking water.

Place the lentils in a pan and cover with cold water. Bring to the boil, then reduce the heat and simmer for 20–25 minutes until the lentils have softened, but retain some texture; drain and set aside until needed.

Heat the olive oil in a casserole dish or Dutch oven over a medium heat. Fry the onion, garlic, celery and rosemary for 2–3 minutes until softened and fragrant. Add the chopped tomatoes. Season with salt, pepper and sugar. Bring to the boil. Add the butternut squash and the reserved soaking water from the dried mushrooms. Cover and cook over a medium heat for 10 minutes, until the squash is tender.

Mix in the soaked mushrooms, chestnut/cremini mushrooms and cooked lentils. Cover and cook for 5 minutes. Check the seasoning. Garnish with parsley and serve at once.

M SMOKED HAM, PUY LENTIL & SQUASH CASSEROLE Omit the fresh mushrooms and add 200 g/7 oz. cubed thick-cut smoked ham to the casserole, stirring it in 5 minutes before the end of cooking time just to heat it through. Serve with creamy mashed potatoes, if liked.

OVEN-BAKED GREEK BUTTER BEANS IN TOMATO SAUCE VE

250 g/1½ cups dried
    gigantes beans, or
    butter/lima beans, soaked
    in water for 24 hours
1 fresh or dried bay leaf
1 large red onion,
    thinly sliced
3 garlic cloves,
    finely chopped
3 tablespoons olive oil
1 teaspoon dried oregano
½ teaspoon ground
    cinnamon
500 g/1 lb 2 oz. vine-ripened
    tomatoes, skinned
    and chopped
2 teaspoons maple syrup
2 tablespoons tomato
    purée/paste
2 tablespoons freshly
    chopped oregano,
    flat-leaf parsley or dill,
    as preferred
salt and freshly ground
    black pepper
extra-virgin olive oil,
    to drizzle
crusty bread, to serve

SERVES 6

The beans in this dish are 'gigantes', aptly named as they are huge dried butter/lima beans that can be up to 4 cm/1½ inches long once they are soaked. Baked in the oven until meltingly soft in a rich, sweet tomato sauce, this is a Greek taverna classic.

Drain the soaked beans (see ingredients), and put in a saucepan with fresh water to cover. Bring to the boil and boil fairly vigorously for 10 minutes, then drain again. With fresh water and the bay leaf, bring back to the boil and simmer very gently for 45 minutes, until the beans are quite tender but not fully cooked. Take off the heat and leave in the liquid.

Preheat the oven to 160°C (325°F) Gas 3.

Gently sauté the onion and garlic in the olive oil in another saucepan, until they soften and smell sweet. Stir in the dried oregano, cinnamon, tomatoes, maple syrup and tomato purée/paste and simmer together for 10 minutes.

Drain the beans, retaining the cooking liquid.

Place the drained beans and tomato sauce in an ovenproof earthenware or cast-iron casserole dish, and stir well. Do not add salt at this stage. Heat the liquid in which the beans have cooked and pour enough of it over the contents of the casserole dish to barely cover the beans.

Bake the casserole, uncovered, in the oven for about 50 minutes, until the beans and the other vegetables are soft and thoroughly cooked, and the sauce is quite thick and concentrated. Check from time to time, and add a little more of the bean cooking liquid or a drizzle of olive oil if necessary to prevent everything drying out, but don't drown it. Season with salt and pepper, stir in the fresh herbs and serve with good crusty bread and extra-virgin olive oil to drizzle over the beans.

V SPICY GREEK BEANS & FETA SAGANAKI-STYLE Prepare as main recipe but substitute runny honey for the maple syrup, if liked. Transfer the beans to a shallow heatproof dish and sprinkle 200 g/7 oz. crumbled feta over the top, add a handful of deseeded and sliced red and/or green fresh chillies/chiles, a sprinkling of dried oregano and a pinch of dried chilli/hot red pepper flakes. Place under a preheated grill/broiler to just melt the cheese and soften the fresh chillies/chiles. Drizzle with extra-virgin olive oil just before serving.

PASTA, NOODLES & RICE

SPICY CRAB SAUCE
WITH QUINOA SPAGHETTI PE

This super quick and easy recipe makes an ideal midweek supper for two people. Quinoa spaghetti is a delicious and more nutritious alternative to wheat pasta and has the additional benefit of being gluten-free.

200 g/7 oz. dried quinoa
    spaghetti
2 garlic cloves, crushed
2 tablespoons olive oil
400-g/14-oz. can chopped
    tomatoes
pinch of dried chilli/
    hot red pepper flakes
80 g/½ cup fresh white
    crab meat
salt and freshly ground
    black pepper
handful of freshly chopped
    flat-leaf parsley,
    to garnish

SERVES 2

Bring a large saucepan or pot of water to the boil over a high heat. Add the quinoa spaghetti to the pan and cook according to the packet instructions.

While the spaghetti is cooking, fry the garlic in the olive oil in a medium–large frying pan/skillet over a medium heat until the garlic just begins to turn brown. Then add the chopped tomatoes and dried chilli/hot red pepper flakes and cook for another few minutes. Reduce the heat and add the crab meat just to warm through.

Drain the spaghetti and put it in the same pan as the sauce. Gently mix the crab and tomato sauce with the spaghetti.

Serve the spaghetti on plates or in large pasta bowls, adding salt and pepper to taste, and garnish with chopped flat-leaf parsley.

VE QUINOA SPAGHETTI WITH SPICY ARTICHOKES Substitute 100 g/3½ oz. canned (or jarred) artichoke hearts for the crab. Drain them of any liquid, cut in half lengthways and then slice finely to create strips. Use in place of the crab, reheating until warmed through.

CREAMY AVOCADO SAUCE
WITH SPELT SPAGHETTI VE

Let's be honest — any dish with avocado in it is delicious! But apart from using it for guacamole and slicing it into salads, it can also be blended with tahini to make a nutritious pasta sauce which only takes a couple of minutes to prepare.

**200 g/7 oz. dried spelt
spaghetti**
1 large ripe avocado
2 tablespoons olive oil
**2 tablespoons umeboshi
vinegar or light soy sauce**
2 tablespoons tahini
**handful of garlic sprouts,
or other seed sprouts**
**2 tablespoons toasted black
sesame seeds, to garnish**

SERVES 2

Bring a large saucepan or pot of water to the boil over a high heat. Add the spelt spaghetti and cook according to the packet instructions. Peel and stone/pit the avocado, then blend along with the olive oil and umeboshi vinegar or soy sauce in a food processor or a blender until smooth. Add a little water if it's very thick. Taste and adjust the seasoning, bearing in mind that it should be on the saltier side, since the pasta needs a strong sauce.

Drain the spaghetti and return it to the hot pan. Pour the avocado sauce over the hot pasta and mix thoroughly. Serve immediately, sprinkling each portion with half of the garlic sprouts (or other sprouts) and add a tablespoon of black sesame seeds, to garnish.

PE AVOCADO & SMOKED SALMON PASTA SAUCE Substitute freshly squeezed lemon juice for the umeboshi vinegar and add 1 peeled garlic clove when blending the avocado in a food processor. Add 100 g/3½ oz. smoked salmon trimmings when you combine the sauce with the hot pasta. To serve, omit the garlic sprouts and black sesame seeds and finish instead with a handful of finely chopped flat-leaf parsley and plenty of freshly ground black pepper.

MAC 'N' CHEESE
WITH MUSHROOMS & HAM

A hearty dish of macaroni cheese is a perennial favourite. Here, the creamy cheese sauce is combined with a tasty mixture of mushrooms and ham.

200 g/2 cups macaroni
or short penne pasta
40 g/3 tablespoons butter
1 bay leaf
40 g/5 tablespoons
plain/all-purpose flour
600 ml/2½ cups
full fat/whole milk
125 g/1¼ cups grated
Cheddar cheese
1 teaspoon wholegrain
mustard
freshly grated nutmeg
1 tablespoon sunflower oil
1 leek, finely chopped
200 g/7 oz. button
mushrooms, halved
100 g/3½ oz. pulled/
shredded or diced
cooked ham
2 tablespoons grated
Parmesan cheese
25 g/⅓ cup fresh
breadcrumbs
1 tablespoon pine nuts
(optional)
salt and freshly ground
black pepper

SERVES 4

Preheat the oven to 200°C (400°F) Gas 6.

Bring a large saucepan of salted water to the boil. Add the pasta and cook according to the package instructions, until slightly underdone; drain and set aside.

Melt the butter with the bay leaf in a heavy-based saucepan. Mix in the flour and cook briefly, stirring. Gradually stir in the milk, mixing well with each addition. Cook, stirring, over a medium heat until the mixture thickens. Stir in the Cheddar cheese until melted. Stir in the mustard and season with nutmeg, salt and black pepper. Turn off the heat and set aside until needed.

Heat the oil in a frying pan/skillet over a low heat. Add the leek and fry gently for 5 minutes until softened, without allowing it to brown. Add the mushrooms, increase the heat, and fry briefly, stirring, until the mushrooms are lightly browned. Season with salt and pepper.

In a large bowl, mix together the cooked macaroni pasta, the mushroom mixture and the pulled/shredded ham. Mix in the cheese sauce. Tip into the shallow baking dish. Sprinkle with the Parmesan cheese, breadcrumbs and pine nuts. Bake in the preheated oven for 30 minutes until golden brown on top. Serve hot.

PE MAC 'N' CHEESE WITH PEAS & TUNA Replace the cooked ham with a 180-g/7-oz. can of tuna in spring water (drained and flaked) and substitute 100 g/¾ cup frozen peas (or petit pois) for the mushrooms and leek. Add the tuna and peas when combining the cheese sauce with the pasta and cook as main recipe but omit the pine nuts when finishing. Finish with a handful of freshly chopped flat-leaf parsley.

V SPICY MAC 'N' CHEESE WITH SWEETCORN & PEPPERS Omit the ham and mushrooms and add 100 g/¾ cup canned sweetcorn/corn kernels, 2 jarred roasted red peppers cut into strips and 2 tablespoons finely chopped green jalapeño peppers. Add the sweetcorn and both the peppers when combining the cheese sauce with the pasta and cook as main recipe. Omit the pine nuts when finishing and dust with a little smoked paprika (optional).

GNOCCHETTI WITH SMOKEY CHORIZO & SEARED PRAWNS Ⓜ

This is a lovely summery pasta dish, perfect for enjoying al fresco — it makes the effort of setting up a table outside completely worthwhile. Its influences are part Italian and part Spanish, which can only mean one thing: it's a tasty little number, just perfect for effortless entertaining.

200 g/7 oz. large raw prawns/jumbo shrimp, peeled and deveined
1 tablespoon red wine vinegar
2 tablespoons olive oil
1 red onion, chopped
1 green (bell) pepper, deseeded and thinly sliced
100 g/3½ oz. chorizo sausage, finely chopped
½ teaspoon Spanish sweet smoked paprika (pimentón dulce)
400-g/14-oz. can chopped tomatoes
300 g/10 oz. dried gnocchetti (or other pasta shape, such as fusilli)
handful of freshly chopped flat-leaf parsley
sea salt and freshly ground black pepper
lemon wedges, to serve

SERVES 4

Put the prawns/shrimp in a non-reactive bowl with the vinegar and 1 tablespoon of the olive oil. Season with a little salt and pepper and set aside. Heat the remaining olive oil in a heavy-based saucepan set over high heat. Add the onion, green pepper and chorizo and cook for 4–5 minutes, until softened and aromatic. Add the paprika and cook for 1 minute, stirring to combine. Add the tomatoes and 125 ml/½ cup water and bring to the boil. Cook for 5 minutes, until the sauce has thickened slightly. Set aside while you cook the pasta.

Bring a large saucepan of lightly salted water to the boil. Add the pasta and cook for 12–15 minutes, until tender yet a little firm to the bite. Drain well and return to the warm pan. Add the tomato sauce and keep warm over very low heat while cooking the prawns/shrimp.

Heat a non-stick frying pan/skiller over high heat. Cook the prawns/shrimp for 2 minutes each side until pink.

Stir the prawns/shrimp through the pasta and season to taste. Spoon onto serving plates and scatter the parsley over each one. Serve with lemon wedges on the side for squeezing.

VE GNOCCHETTI WITH BUTTER BEANS & VEGGIE CHORIZO Substitute 200 g/1 cup canned butter/lima beans for the prawns/shrimp and replace the chorizo with 150 g/6 oz. of store-bought meat-free chorizo (available as chunks or slices from brands such as Cheatin') or pepperoni slices (such as Quorn). Prepare the sauce as main recipe, adding the drained and rinsed beans and chorizo for a few minutes at the end of cooking time just to warm them through. Stir into the drained pasta and serve garnished with the flat-leaf parsley.

THAI-STYLE VEGETABLES
EN PAPILLOTE WITH NOODLES VE

4 carrots, finely chopped into matchsticks

2 shallots, finely sliced

2 pak choi/bok choy, leaves separated and centres halved

1 mooli/daikon radish, peeled and finely sliced or 14–16 red radishes, finely sliced

2 large red chillies/chiles, finely sliced on the diagonal

50 g/½ cup roughly chopped galangal or ginger in 2-cm/¾-inch pieces

2 lemon grass stalks, bruised and sliced into 2-cm/¾-inch pieces

150 g/1⅓ cup trimmed and chopped green beans in 2.5-cm/1-inch pieces

100 ml/⅓ cup rice wine

8 okra, trimmed and sliced into 5-mm/¼-inch pieces

100 g/3½ oz. shiitake mushrooms, stems removed and quartered

good splash of sesame oil

600 g/1 lb 5 oz. pre-cooked medium noodles

vegetable oil, for frying

TO SERVE
dark soy sauce

small bunch of fresh coriander/cilantro

cashew nuts, crushed

SERVES 4

This is a lovely fusion dish, taking the classic Pad Thai as its inspiration, but baked in paper to make the most of the perfumed aromas from the rice wine, aromatic lemon grass and galangal root.

Preheat the oven to 180°C (350°F) Gas 4.

To make a papillote bag, cut a rectangle of baking parchment approximately 30 x 45 cm/12 x 18 inches and a piece of foil 40 x 55 cm/ 16 x 22 inches. Place the baking parchment on top of the foil and fold in half. Seal the sides by folding the foil over several times, capturing the baking parchment inside, forming an envelope.

Carefully place the carrots, shallots, pak choi/bok choy, daikon radish or red radishes, chillies/chiles, galangal or ginger, lemon grass and green beans inside the envelope and add the rice wine. Seal the top and put on a baking sheet. Bake in the preheated oven for 20 minutes.

To prepare the noodles preheat a large frying pan/skillet over a high heat with just enough vegetable oil to coat the bottom. When the oil is just starting to shimmer from the heat, add the okra and mushrooms. Cook for 3 minutes, turning occasionally, until the okra is starting to turn golden. Add a good splash of sesame oil and then the noodles. Reduce the heat to low and turn the noodles in the pan to warm them through and mix with the okra and mushrooms.

To serve, place the papillote bag in a large bowl and rest for 5 minutes (don't serve the lemon grass or galangal or ginger pieces). Put the noodles in another large bowl and dress with a little soy sauce. Put the coriander/ cilantro leaves and cashew nuts in smaller serving bowls. When you open the papillote bag at the table, it will fill the room with wonderful aromas.

Allow your guests to help themselves for the perfect balance.

PE AROMATIC COD EN PAPILLOTE WITH SESAME BEANS Assemble the parcels as main recipe but add a 125-g/4½-oz. skinless and boneless cod fillet to each parcel. Reduce the cooking time in the preheated oven to 12–15 minutes. Garnish the cooked fish with freshly chopped coriander/cilantro and replace the noodles with a side of steamed green beans, tossed in 2 teaspoons of sesame oil and sprinkled with toasted sesame seeds.

SOBA NOODLE BOWL WITH PAK CHOI, CASHEWS & TAMARI SAUCE VE

This is a great go-to Asian dish when only a bowl of noodles will do! Soba noodles are made from buckwheat flour so make a good alternative to egg noodles.

50 g/½ cup cashew nuts
340 g/12 oz. buckwheat (soba) noodles
1 onion, chopped
1 tablespoon finely chopped fresh ginger
1 tablespoon grapeseed oil
200-g/7-oz. (1 large head) pak choi/bok choy, chopped

TAMARI SAUCE

1 tablespoon soy sauce
2 teaspoons sesame oil
¼ teaspoon finely chopped ginger
2 teaspoons linseed/ flaxseed oil
2 teaspoons maple syrup or agave syrup, as preferred
1 tablespoon freshly squeezed lemon juice
1 tablespoon white sesame seeds

SERVES 4

Roast the cashews by scattering them on an ungreased baking sheet and cooking in a preheated oven at 180°C (350°F) Gas 4 for 10 minutes, or until golden. Set aside until needed.

Prepare the tamari sauce in advance. Whisk all of the ingredients together in the base of a large bowl until combined.

Cook the noodles in salted water in a large saucepan or pot over a medium heat for 10–12 minutes, or according to the packet instructions.

In a large frying pan/skillet, fry the onion and ginger in the grapeseed oil until the onion is translucent. Add the chopped pak choi/bok choy, and cook until wilted.

Drain the noodles, then mix together with the fried vegetables in the reserved bowl of tamari sauce.

Toss with chopped roasted cashew nuts and serve.

PE BUCKWHEAT NOODLES WITH PAN-FRIED SALMON & PAK CHOI Prepare the noodles and Tamari Sauce as main recipe but reserve a little of the sauce to dress the salmon. Take 4 x 150-g/5½-oz. boneless salmon fillets and season with salt and black pepper. Heat 2 tablespoons of oil in a large frying pan/skillet and fry the salmon skin-side down for 2–3 minutes, then turn over and fry for a further 1–2 minutes, or until cooked through. Place the salmon skin-side up on top of a bowl of the warm noodles and spoon the reserved dressing over each serving.

BEETROOT RISOTTO

A risotto is a great staple for everyday eating. This simple vegan recipe
is particularly tasty and its colour will always be a conversation point too.

500 g/1 lb 2 oz. raw
  beetroot/beets
  (about 2 medium–large)
2 teaspoons olive oil
2 red onions, finely chopped
2 garlic cloves, crushed
6–8-cm/2½–3-inch piece
  of fresh ginger, peeled
  and grated
400 g/generous 2 cups
  risotto rice, such as
  Arborio
200 ml/1 scant cup vegan
  white wine
850 ml/3½ cups vegetable
  stock
grated zest and freshly
  squeezed juice of
  1–2 lemons, to taste
3 fresh thyme sprigs,
  leaves finely chopped
salt and freshly ground
  black pepper
freshly chopped flat-leaf
  parsley, to serve

SERVES 4

Preheat the oven to 200°C (400°F) Gas 6.

Individually wrap the beetroot/beets in kitchen foil and put them
on a baking sheet. Bake in the preheated oven for about 40 minutes,
or until tender. Set aside until cool enough to handle, then rub off
the skin using the foil and cut the beetroot/beets into cubes. Set aside.

Heat the olive oil in a heavy-based saucepan, add the onions and
cook over a low heat for about 10 minutes until soft but not coloured.
Add 2 tablespoons of water to the pan if the onions are sticking. Stir
in the garlic and ginger and cook for 1–2 minutes. Add the rice and
cook until it turns opaque. Add the wine and stir until absorbed. Add
a quarter of the stock and stir until all the liquid has been absorbed.

Continue to add the stock in stages, stirring constantly until the rice
is soft but still has bite. Remove from the heat, then stir in the lemon
zest and juice. Next stir in the beetroot/beet and thyme, and season
with salt and pepper. The consistency should be thick and creamy;
add additional stock if required.

Spoon into warmed serving bowls and sprinkle with the chopped
parsley. Serve immediately.

V **BEETROOT & FETA RISOTTO WITH MINT** Prepare the risotto as main recipe.
Add 100 g/3½ oz. crumbled feta to the warm risotto and stir in until molten. Omit the fresh
thyme and parsley and add some freshly chopped mint leaves as a garnish just before serving.

PE **BEETROOT & SMOKED MACKEREL RISOTTO WITH HORSERADISH
CREAM** Prepare the risotto as main recipe. Take 140 g/5 oz. boneless hot smoked mackerel
fillets. Remove the skin, break the fish into chunky pieces and fold these into the cooked risotto.
Spoon into serving bowls. Mix 1 tablespoon of horseradish sauce with 3 tablespoons of crème
fraîche or sour cream and swirl a spoonful of this mixture into each serving.

SPICED ALMOND PILAF VE

Delicately flavoured with fragrant spices, this nutty basmati rice dish is delicious on its own as a light vegan main, or served as an accompaniment to other dishes.

1½ tablespoons vegetable oil
1 shallot, finely chopped
1 cinnamon stick
2 cardamom pods
200 g/1 cup basmati rice, rinsed
1 tablespoon tomato purée/paste
225 g/8 oz. ripe tomatoes
25 g/3 tablespoons flaked/slivered almonds, dry-fried until golden
freshly chopped coriander/cilantro, to garnish
salt

SERVES 4

Heat the oil in a heavy-bottomed saucepan set over a medium heat. Add the shallot, cinnamon stick and cardamom pods and fry gently, stirring now and then, for 2 minutes, until the shallot softens.

Mix in the basmati rice, coating well with the oil, then the tomato purée/paste. Pour over 300 ml/1¼ cups of water and season with salt. Bring the mixture to the boil, reduce the heat, cover and simmer for 10–15 minutes, until the water has all been absorbed and the rice is tender.

Meanwhile, scald the tomatoes. Pour boiling water over the tomatoes in a small pan or pot set over a medium heat. Heat for 1 minute, then remove from the water and carefully peel off the skin using a sharp knife. Halve the tomatoes, scoop out the soft pulp and finely dice the tomato shells.

When the rice is cooked, transfer to a serving dish. Fold in the diced tomatoes, sprinkle with the flaked/slivered almonds and coriander/cilantro, and serve at once.

M ROAST LEMON & SUMAC CHICKEN WITH TOMATO PILAF Take 6–8 chicken thighs, rinse and pat dry with paper towels. Preheat the oven to 180°C (350°F) Gas 4. Put the freshly squeezed juice of half a lemon, 1 tablespoon of sumac, 4 crushed garlic cloves, 1 teaspoon salt and 2 tablespoons olive oil in a large bowl. Add the chicken thighs and toss to cover in the marinade. Slice an unwaxed lemon and lay it in a baking dish. Lay the chicken skin-side up over the top. Roast, uncovered, in the preheated oven for about 30–40 minutes, until cooked. The juice should run clear when you pierce a thigh. Serve hot with the pilaf on the side.

CATALAN RICE WITH SMOKED HADDOCK & ROASTED PEPPERS PE

Based on a traditional Spanish recipe, this rice dish gets both its unique flavour and colour from saffron. Simply omit the fish for a tasty vegetarian option.

300 g/10 oz. undyed smoked haddock fillet
400-g/14-oz. can chickpeas, drained and rinsed
generous pinch of saffron strands
1 red (bell) pepper, halved lengthways and deseeded
2 large tomatoes
3 tablespoons olive oil
6 garlic cloves, finely chopped
250 g/1¼ cups short-grain rice, such as Bomba or Arborio
2 hard-boiled/hard-cooked eggs, peeled and cut into quarters

SERVES 4

Poach the smoked haddock gently in water for 5 minutes and drain. Flake the fish with a fork, removing any stray bones, and set aside.

Warm the chickpeas in a little water, crumbling the strands of saffron into the pan. Simmer very gently for about 20 minutes so that they take on the colour and flavour of the saffron. Drain through a sieve/strainer, reserving the saffron-infused cooking water, and set both aside.

Put the red (bell) pepper halves under a preheated grill/broiler, skin-side up, until the skins blacken. Transfer to a plastic bag for a few minutes, then lift off the blackened skins and slice the flesh into strips.

Blanch the tomatoes in boiling water for 1 minute, peel, deseed and chop the flesh.

Heat the olive oil in a large saucepan and cook the garlic gently for 1–2 minutes, until it becomes golden, being careful not to burn it. Add the tomato pulp and cook for another 5 minutes or so, until it has disintegrated, and then tip the rice into the pan and stir thoroughly until every grain is coated. Add 600 ml/2½ cups of water (including the reserved saffron-infused water) and bring to the boil. Simmer for 20 minutes, uncovered, until the rice is cooked and no liquid remains.

Stir in the chickpeas and flaked fish, heat through for a few minutes, then strew the strips of red (bell) pepper over. Place the hard-boiled/hard-cooked egg quarters on top and serve.

***

VE SPANISH-STYLE SAFFRON RICE WITH PAPRIKA HEARTS OF PALM

Prepare the rice as main recipe omitting the smoked haddock and eggs and keep warm until ready to serve. Take a 400-g/14-oz. can of hearts of palm. Drain and slice into 1.5-cm/½-inch slices. Lay these on paper towels to absorb their moisture and sprinkle with ½ teaspoon of Spanish smoked paprika and season with salt and pepper. Heat 1 tablespoon of vegetable oil over a medium-high heat until very hot. Add to the hot pan, seasoned-side down, and sprinkle with another ½ teaspoon of smoked paprika and season again. Cook for 1–2 minutes on each side, or until starting to brown. Remove from the heat and arrange on top of each serving of rice. Serve with a simple aioli made by blending a crushed garlic clove with 4 tablespoons of store-bought vegan mayonnaise and add a spoonful to the top of each serving (optional).

***

VEGETABLE JAMBALAYA VE

Jambalaya may have its origins in Spanish paella, but here, it has added heat with chilli/chile and smokey flavour with paprika. Roasting the okra and broccoli gives it a wonderful nutty flavour and a crisp texture.

1 green (bell) pepper, deseeded and finely diced

1 red (bell) pepper, deseeded and finely diced

4 sticks/ribs celery, thinly sliced

2 onions, finely diced

2 teaspoons smoked Spanish paprika

2 fresh red chillies/chiles, thinly sliced

500 g/2½ cups short-grain rice, such as Bomba or Arborio

1 litre/quart vegetable stock

100 g/½ cup frozen peas

50 g/⅓ cup frozen sweetcorn kernels

100 g/3½ oz. fresh okra, trimmed and halved lengthways

100 g/3½ oz. broccoli florets

100 g/1 heaped cup mangetout/snow peas or sugarsnap beans, trimmed

4 tomatoes, quartered

salt

vegetable oil, for frying and roasting

SERVES 4

Preheat the oven to 180°C (350°F) Gas 4.

In a large saucepan, cover the base with vegetable oil and bring to a moderate temperature over a medium heat. Add the (bell) peppers, celery, onions and smoked paprika and allow them to cook for a few minutes, stirring regularly, until the vegetables are starting to turn golden and catch on the base of the pan. Add the chillies/chiles, then the rice and stir to just coat the rice with the oil. Now add the stock and a level teaspoon of table salt and bring to a low simmer. Continue to simmer for 10 minutes.

Add the frozen peas and sweetcorn, and bring back to a simmer. Continue to simmer for another 5 minutes, until the rice is cooked.

While the rice is cooking, put the okra and broccoli on a baking sheet, drizzle with oil and add a good sprinkle of salt. Toss to coat evenly, then roast them in the preheated oven for 10 minutes.

Once the rice is cooked, add the mangetout/snow peas or sugarsnap beans and tomatoes, and stir through.

Serve the rice onto warm plates and place the roasted okra and broccoli on top to finish the jambalaya.

PE **JAMBALAYA WITH PAN-FRIED GARLIC PRAWNS** Prepare the jambalaya as main recipe but omit the fresh chilli/chile. Keep warm until ready to serve. Gently melt 25 g/2 tablespoons butter with 2 tablespoons olive oil in a frying pan/skillet. Add 3 cloves of chopped garlic, 1 finely chopped fresh red chilli/chile (leaving the seeds in for extra heat). Fry for 1–2 minutes until the garlic is just turning brown. Turn up the heat, add 12–20 shell-on raw king prawns/jumbo shrimp to the pan and fry until they turn pink. Remove from the heat, season with salt and pepper and stir in the freshly squeezed juice of 1 lemon plus a handful of freshly chopped flat-leaf parsley. Divide the hot prawns/shrimp between each serving.

ASPARAGUS RISOTTO Ⓥ

4 carrots, peeled
2 celery sticks/ribs
3 onions
400 g/14 oz. fresh asparagus
80 g/1¼ cups baby spinach
  leaves, washed
2 garlic cloves, finely sliced
350 g/2 cups Arborio rice
200 ml/1 scant cup white
  wine
80 g/1¼ cup grated
  vegetarian Parmesan
  cheese
grated zest of ½ lemon
a knob/pat of butter
salt
olive oil, for frying

SERVES 4

This creamy and rich recipe is a great way to enjoy the flavour of asparagus, and the dramatic appearance of a vibrant green risotto makes it great fun, too.

To make an asparagus stock, finely dice the carrots, celery and 2 of the onions and put in a large saucepan with 1 litre/quart of water.

Trim about 2.5 cm/1 inch from the base of the asparagus spears and discard. Trim a further 2.5 cm/1 inch from the base of the spears, finely slice them and place in the stock water. Bring the stock to a low simmer and cook for 45 minutes. Add the spinach and simmer for 2 minutes, then blend the stock with a handheld electric blender until smooth.

Add a little oil to a large heavy-based non-stick saucepan. Finely dice the remaining onion and add to the pan with the garlic and cook over a very low heat until just translucent. Add the rice and cook, gently stirring, until the rice is covered with oil and starts to go opaque. Add the wine and simmer until the wine is nearly all absorbed. Stirring constantly, add half of the asparagus stock and a pinch of salt and continue cooking on a low simmer until all of the stock is absorbed. Continue adding the remaining stock a little at a time until the rice is cooked and has just a little bite when tasted (there should be no excess liquid).

To finish, beat in the Parmesan cheese, lemon zest and a knob/ pat of butter to loosen the risotto. Add the asparagus and serve.

VE ASPARAGUS & PEA RISOTTO Prepare as main recipe, adding a handful of frozen petit pois with the last ladle of asparagus stock. Replace the wine with vegan wine, omit the vegetarian Parmesan and use a little olive oil to loosen the risotto in place of the butter. Finish each serving with a sprinkle of Vegan Parmesan (see page 8).

M ASPARAGUS RISOTTO WITH PROSCIUTTO Prepare as main recipe. Cut 3 slices of Prosciutto into strips and stir them into the rice along with the asparagus tips.

OVEN BAKES
& SHEET PANS

BUTTERNUT & CAULIFLOWER LENTIL KORMA VE

This is a very cost-effective and colourful vegan tray bake, combining sweet but not too starchy butternut squash and cauliflower with lentils and spices and coconut milk. It is a mild curry that will tempt reluctant vegans!

2 red onions, cut into quarters
400 g/14 oz. butternut squash, peeled, deseeded and cut into 1-cm/½-inch cubes
½ cauliflower, cut into florets
2 teaspoons olive oil
60 g/¼ cup korma curry paste
200 ml/scant 1 cup coconut milk
400-g/14-oz. can green lentils, drained and rinsed
1 lemon, cut into quarters, to serve
1 tablespoon freshly chopped coriander/cilantro, to serve

SERVES 2

Preheat the oven to 200°C (400°F) Gas 6.

Put the onions, butternut squash and cauliflower in a sheet pan with sides and drizzle over the olive oil.

Bake in the preheated oven for 30–35 minutes until all the vegetables are soft and the cauliflower is also brown and crispy at the edges.

Meanwhile, mix the curry paste and coconut milk together. Pour the mixture over the vegetables and stir in the lentils.

Bake for a further 10 minutes. Squeeze over the lemon quarters, sprinkle over the coriander/cilantro and serve.

V CURRIED VEGETABLE SHEET PAN WITH PANEER & NIGELLA SEEDS

Add 225 g/8 oz. paneer (Indian firm cheese), cut into 2-cm/¾-inch cubes. Toss the cubes with the vegetables and cook as main recipe. Add a sprinkling of nigella seeds after you add the curry paste mixture and before returning to the oven.

STUFFED MUSHROOMS

A perfect example of no-waste cooking, this recipe makes use of the stalks of the mushrooms to stuff the caps, along with breadcrumbs and fragrant basil pesto.

4 large, even-sized field/
meadow mushrooms,
each approx. 9-cm/
3½-inch diameter
100 g/1⅓ cups fresh
breadcrumbs
3 tablespoons store-bought
fresh basil pesto
3 tablespoons olive oil
25 g/⅓ cup grated
vegetarian Parmesan
cheese
2 tablespoons pine nuts
salt and freshly ground
black pepper

SERVES 4

Preheat the oven to 200°C (400°F) Gas 6.

Trim the stalks off the mushrooms and finely chop. Mix together the chopped stalks, breadcrumbs, pesto, 2 tablespoons olive oil, Parmesan cheese and pine nuts.

Brush the skin side of the mushroom caps lightly with olive oil. Place skin-side down on a baking sheet. Season the inside of the mushroom caps with salt and pepper. Fill each mushroom cap with the pesto mixture, pressing it in firmly. Drizzle the surface of the filled mushrooms with the remaining olive oil.

Bake in the preheated oven for 20 minutes and serve at once.

VE SAGE & WALNUT PESTO MUSHROOMS WITH CRANBERRIES Blend 15 g/1 cup fresh sage, 15 g/1 cup fresh flat-leaf parsley, 3 cloves garlic and 130 g/1 cup toasted walnuts in a food processor for 15 seconds. Add 2 tablespoons freshly squeezed lemon juice and pour 125 ml/½ cup olive oil through the pour spout at the top. Finish by blending in up to 65 ml/¼ cup water to achieve the desired consistency. Prepare and cook as main recipe, adding 2 tablespoons of dried cranberries to the mushroom mixture in the frying pan/skillet and substituting the sage and walnut pesto for the basil pesto. Add a sprinkling of chopped walnuts to each filled mushroom before baking.

CHEESY LENTIL BAKE

This thrifty and humble recipe dates from the Second World War, when rationing was in force and meat was scarce. It will emerge from the oven with a deliciously crisp and golden top. Serve with a side of broccoli or green beans, if liked.

300 g/1½ cups dried
  red lentils
30 g/2 tablespoons butter
1 onion, chopped
900 ml/3¾ cups milk
125 g/4 oz. Cheddar cheese,
  grated
2 tablespoons fresh
  breadcrumbs
salt and freshly ground
  black pepper

a 1-litre/quart capacity
  gratin dish, well buttered

SERVES 4

Rinse the lentils and soak in cold water for 1 hour, then drain. Melt the butter in a medium-sized saucepan, and fry the onion very gently until soft and beginning to brown. This will take about 15 minutes.

Next, pour the milk into the pan and add the drained lentils, then stir around and bring to the boil. Once it has boiled, turn down the heat and simmer, uncovered, until the lentils are soft, which will take about an hour. Stir the mixture from time to time to prevent it sticking to the bottom of the pan, and if the liquid seems to be evaporating too fast, half-cover the pan, or top up with a little hot water, but don't let the mixture become too sloppy. It should be the texture of loose porridge/oatmeal when it is cooked.

Preheat the oven to 180°C (350°F) Gas 4.

When the lentils are cooked, season to taste with a little salt – don't overdo the salt as the cheese is salty – and pepper. Stir in half of the grated cheese.

Spoon the lentil and cheese mixture into the prepared gratin dish. Mix together the breadcrumbs and remaining cheese, then sprinkle over the top. Bake in the preheated oven for about 20–30 minutes, until the top is nicely crisp and golden. Serve immediately.

M CHEESE & BACON LENTILS WITH POACHED EGGS Roughly chop 4 rashers/slices streaky bacon and add to the frying pan/skillet with the onion and cook as main recipe. Top each serving with a poached egg and a few dashes of a hot sauce, such as Tabasco, if liked.

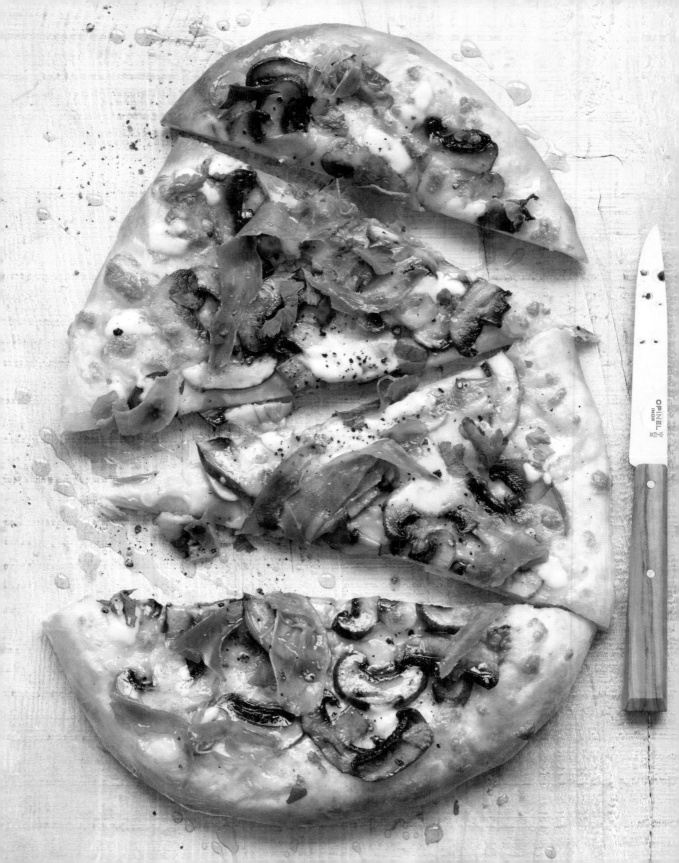

TRUFFLED MUSHROOM & PARMA HAM PIZZA (M)

Making pizza from scratch is very satisfying. It also means that you can be creative with the toppings! The additions of Parma ham and a touch of truffle oil make for a stylish take on a mushroom pizza.

500 g/4 cups strong white/bread flour
1 teaspoon fast-action dried yeast
1 teaspoon salt
½ teaspoon sugar
250–275 ml/1–1¼ cups warm water
3½ tablespoons olive oil
500 g/1 lb 2 oz. white/cup mushrooms, sliced 5 mm/¼-inch thick
1 garlic clove, chopped
2 balls of mozzarella cheese, torn into pieces
4 slices of Parma ham/ prosciutto, roughly torn
a handful of freshly chopped flat-leaf parsley
1 teaspoon truffle oil
salt and freshly ground black pepper

SERVES 4

First, make the pizza dough. Place the flour, yeast, salt and sugar in a large bowl and mix together. Gradually mix in the warm water to form a soft, sticky dough. Knead the dough on a floured surface for 10 minutes, until smooth and supple.

Place the dough in a floured bowl, cover with a clean kitchen cloth or cling film/plastic wrap. Set aside in a warm place for 1 hour to rise, until the dough has doubled in size.

Preheat the oven to 250°C (475°F) Gas 9. Place 2 baking sheets in the oven to heat.

Heat a large, heavy frying pan/skillet. Add 1 tablespoon of the olive oil, heat through, then add the mushrooms. Fry over a high heat for 8 minutes, stirring now and then, until any liquid from the mushrooms has evaporated and they are lightly browned.

Add a further ½ tablespoon olive oil and heat through. Add the garlic to the oil and fry, stirring, for 1 minute. Season with salt and pepper. Set aside.

Divide the risen dough into 4 equal-sized portions. Roll out each portion on a lightly floured, clean work surface, to form a circular pizza base. Brush each pizza base evenly with ½ tablespoon of the olive oil. Sprinkle each with the fried mushrooms, dividing them evenly among the 4 bases. Dot with mozzarella pieces.

Transfer to the baking sheets, then bake in batches if necessary, in the preheated oven for 10 minutes until the dough is golden-brown.

Top the pizzas with Parma ham/prosciutto and sprinkle with parsley. Drizzle ¼ tablespoon truffle oil over each pizza, if using. Serve at once.

VE MUSHROOM, ARTICHOKE, OLIVE & CAPER PIZZA Prepare the dough and mushrooms as main recipe. Omit the Parma ham and replace with 4 chargrilled and marinated artichoke hearts, 6 pitted and halved black olives and 1 tablespoon capers. Replace the mozzarella with a handful of vegan mozzarella-style cheese (optional). Add a handful of shredded basil to the finished pizza and drizzle with extra-virgin oil, in place of the truffle oil.

LENTIL MOUSSAKA

500 g/1 lb 2 oz.
   aubergines/eggplants
about 6 tablespoons
   olive oil
1 onion, finely chopped
1 leek, trimmed and
   chopped
3 garlic cloves, chopped
1 carrot, peeled and
   finely diced
6 tomatoes (about
   750 g/1 lb 10 oz.),
   peeled and chopped
4 tablespoons tomato
   purée/paste
½ teaspoon ground
   cinnamon
1 tablespoon dried oregano
2 fresh or dried bay leaves
1 teaspoon caster/
   granulated sugar
200 g/1 cup dried Puy/
   French green lentils
200 g/2 cups grated
   vegetarian Pecorino-style
   cheese
salt and freshly ground
   black pepper

TOPPING
3 eggs, beaten
30 g/¼ cup plain/
   all-purpose flour
500 ml/2¼ cups natural/
   plain thick Greek yogurt
a pinch of freshly grated
   nutmeg
salt and freshly ground
   black pepper

*a 28 x 18-cm/11 x 7-inch
ovenproof dish,
generously buttered*

SERVES 6

This is a vegetarian version of a retro dish that normally includes minced/ground beef or lamb. It makes a good supper dish, served with a crisp green salad and some good bread.

Preheat the oven to 180°C (350°F) Gas 4.

Cut the aubergines/eggplants into 1-cm/⅜-inch slices, and brush the cut sides with olive oil. Heat a baking sheet with sides in the oven for 5 minutes, then bake the aubergine/eggplant slices, sprinkled with a little salt, for about 30 minutes, until beginning to brown. Halfway through cooking, turn them over with a spatula, so they cook evenly.

Meanwhile, heat 3 tablespoons of the olive oil in a frying pan/skillet and fry the onion, leek and garlic over a gentle heat until soft and golden. Add the diced carrot, chopped tomatoes, tomato purée/paste, cinnamon, oregano and bay leaves, cover and simmer together for another 30 minutes or so. Stir in the sugar.

While the tomato sauce is cooking, rinse and drain the lentils, then place in a saucepan covered with cold water. Bring to the boil and simmer for about 20 minutes, until soft (bear in mind that they will not cook any further once mixed with the tomato sauce.) Drain the lentils and add to the tomato sauce, then season with salt and pepper.

Spread half of the aubergine/eggplant slices in the bottom of the prepared ovenproof dish. Cover with half of the tomato and lentil mixture, then repeat with another layer of each. Sprinkle half of the grated cheese over the surface.

To make the topping, whisk the eggs with the flour, then gently stir in the yogurt, 1 level teaspoon salt and some pepper and the grated nutmeg. Spoon this mixture over the dish of vegetables, finishing by sprinkling the remaining grated cheese over the surface.

Bake in the preheated oven for 30–40 minutes, until the top is bubbling and brown. Serve hot.

VE LENTIL & AUBERGINE BAKE WITH OLIVE OIL MASH Make the filling as main recipe but omit the grated Pecorino and the topping. Peel 800 g/1 lb 12 oz. floury potatoes and cut them into chunks. Cover with salted water in a large saucepan and add 2 peeled garlic cloves. Boil until tender, drain and mash with 2 tablespoons good olive oil. Season generously with salt and freshly ground black pepper. Spoon over the dish of filling, level the surface and bake as main recipe. Sprinkle with freshly chopped flat-leaf parsley to serve.

AUBERGINE LASAGNE

This is a great vegetarian take on a much-loved classic pasta dish, this is delicious home-cooked food with that magical Italian touch.

AUBERGINE FILLING
5 tablespoons olive oil
1 onion, chopped
1 garlic clove, chopped
1 kg/2 lb 4 oz. ripe
    tomatoes, scalded,
    skinned and chopped
    (reserve any juices),
    see page 105
handful of fresh basil
    leaves, roughly chopped
2 aubergines/eggplants,
    finely diced
about 12 lasagne sheets,
    cooked according to the
    package instructions
25 g/⅓ cup freshly grated
    vegetarian Parmesan
    cheese
salt and freshly ground
    black pepper

WHITE SAUCE
25 g/2 tablespoons butter
25 g/3½ tablespoons
    plain/all-purpose flour
300 ml/1¼ cups milk
pinch of freshly grated
    nutmeg

*a 28 x 18-cm/11 x 7-inch
    ovenproof dish,
    generously oiled*

SERVES 4

Heat 1 tablespoon of the oil in a large, heavy-bottomed frying pan/ skillet over a low heat. Fry the onion and garlic until softened. Add the chopped tomatoes with their juices. Season with salt and pepper.

Increase the heat, cover and bring the mixture to the boil. Uncover and cook for a further 5 minutes, stirring often, until reduced and thickened. Stir in the basil.

Heat 2 tablespoons of the oil in a separate large, heavy-bottomed frying pan/skillet set over a medium heat. Add half of the diced aubergine/ eggplant and fry, stirring often, until softened and lightly browned, then set aside. Repeat the process with the remaining oil and aubergine/ eggplant. Mix the fried aubergine/eggplant into the tomato sauce.

Preheat the oven to 200°C (400°F) Gas 6.

Make the white sauce by melting the butter in a heavy-bottomed saucepan or pot set over a low–medium heat. Stir in the flour and cook, stirring, for 1–2 minutes. Gradually pour in the milk, stirring continuously to combine. Bring the mixture to the boil and simmer until thickened. Season with salt, pepper and nutmeg.

Arrange a layer of cooked lasagne sheets in the prepared ovenproof dish. Put a layer of the aubergine/eggplant mixture over the top, then sprinkle over a little vegetarian Parmesan cheese. Repeat the process, finishing with a layer of lasagne sheets. Spread the white sauce evenly over the top, then sprinkle over the remaining vegetarian Parmesan.

Bake in the preheated oven for 40–50 minutes until golden-brown. Remove from the oven and serve at once.

M BEEF LASAGNE Omit the Aubergine Filling. Heat 1 tablespoon olive oil in a large saucepan over a low heat. Add 1 finely chopped onion and sauté for 10 minutes, or until soft. Turn up the heat and add 2 crushed garlic cloves and 400 g/14 oz. lean beef mince. Fry for 5 minutes, stirring frequently. Add 200 g/7 oz. roughly chopped mushrooms and cook for 5 minutes. Add a 400-g/14-oz. can of tomatoes, 1 tablespoon tomato purée/paste, 1 tablespoon dried mixed herbs and a few dashes of Worcestershire sauce. Season, bring to the boil, simmer for 15 minutes, stirring occasionally. Remove from the heat. Substitute this mixture for the Aubergine Filling as you prepare and cook the lasagne following the main recipe.

FENNEL & ROAST
TOMATO LASAGNE ⬣ v

A delicious and sophisticated vegetarian twist on an Italian classic.
Serve with sweet potato chips/fries for a satisfying meal.

3 fennel bulbs, thinly sliced
800 g/1 lb 12 oz. tomatoes
    on the vine
2 tablespoons olive oil
2 tablespoons balsamic
    vinegar
300 ml/1¼ cups
    double/heavy cream
100 g/1⅓ cups grated
    vegetarian Parmesan
    cheese
about 12 lasagne sheets,
    cooked according to the
    package instructions
salt and freshly ground
    black pepper

a 28 x 18-cm/11 x 7-inch
    ovenproof dish,
    generously oiled

SERVES 4

Preheat the oven to 180°C (350°F) Gas 4.

Spread the sliced fennel out on a roasting pan, drizzle with olive oil
and sprinkle with a pinch of salt and pepper.

Put the tomatoes (still on the vine) on a separate baking sheet, drizzle
with the olive oil and balsamic vinegar and season with a pinch of salt
and a little freshly ground black pepper.

Put both sheets in the preheated oven and cook for 30 minutes.

Remove the fennel, pour over the cream, mix with the fennel, and
return to the oven for a further 10 minutes.

Transfer the tomatoes to a large mixing bowl. Carefully remove the
vine and lightly crush the tomatoes with the back of a fork. Leave the
oven on.

Add most of the cheese to the fennel and cream mixture and stir,
making a thick cheesy sauce with a custard-like consistency.

In the prepared ovenproof dish, start to assemble the lasagne with a
thin layer of tomatoes, then a layer of lasagne sheets, followed by a layer
of fennel and another layer of lasagne sheets. Continue with this pattern
of layers; tomatoes, pasta, fennel, pasta, finishing with fennel, onto which
you can sprinkle the remaining cheese. Cover with foil and set aside.

Remove the foil from the lasagne for the last 10 minutes of cooking
to allow the top to brown.

Remove from the oven and serve.

PE SALMON & FENNEL LASAGNE To turn this into a luxurious fish dish take
2 fillets (about 170 g/6 oz.) of hot smoked salmon. Break the flesh into chunks and place them
in between the tomatoes when adding this layer. (As the salmon is pre-cooked you don't need
to adjust the cooking time.) If you find you have a few leftover roasted tomatoes, simply purée
them in a blender, season and serve on the side as a spooning sauce.

OVEN-ROASTED ROOTS VE

This dish may take a little bit of preparation but the end result is a beautiful plate of food with each vegetable cooked to its full, delicious potential.

4 carrots, unpeeled
1 star anise
4 large potatoes, peeled and cut in half
4 parsnips, peeled and cut into quarters lengthways
pinch of cumin seeds
drizzle of maple syrup
1 celeriac/celery root, peeled and diced into 1-cm/³/₈-inch cubes
1 small pumpkin, unpeeled and sliced into 2-cm/ ³/₄-inch wedges
1 large sweet potato, peeled and sliced into 2-cm/ ³/₄-inch rounds
1 teaspoon miso paste
2 onions, trimmed and quartered
a handful of fresh marjoram, thyme and sage leaves
salt and ground white pepper
vegetable oil, to coat

SERVES 4

Preheat the oven to 180°C (350°F) Gas 4.

Scrub the carrots with a wire scourer to clean off all the dirt and make them rough. Put in a saucepan of cold salted water and add the star anise. Set over a medium heat and bring to a low simmer for 10 minutes, then remove from the water using a slotted spoon and leave to cool. Slice in half lengthways, rub with a little vegetable oil and place on a sheet pan with a light covering of salt to season, leaving room for all the other vegetables.

Put the potatoes in a saucepan of cold salted water. Set over a medium heat and bring to a low simmer for about 15 minutes until they are just starting to flake and break up. Drain the potatoes using a fine mesh sieve/ strainer and set over the warm pan (no longer on the heat) for 10 minutes to dry out completely. Toss with a little oil and add a pinch of salt and white pepper while they are still warm. Transfer to the sheet pan with the carrots.

Rub a little vegetable oil over the parsnips and then a little maple syrup to form a thin glaze. Put on the sheet pan and sprinkle with a little salt to season. Toss the celeriac/celery root cubes with some vegetable oil and ½ teaspoon of salt and transfer to the sheet pan.

Remove any seeds from the pumpkin slices, rub with vegetable oil to coat, then sprinkle lightly with cumin seeds. Transfer to the sheet pan and arrange skin-side down. Rub the sweet potato slices with vegetable oil, then rub the flesh with the miso paste. Transfer to the sheet pan. Add the onion and drizzle with a little vegetable oil.

Sprinkle a few marjoram, sage and thyme leaves over the top and cook in the preheated oven for 30–40 minutes or until the potatoes are golden brown. Remove from the oven and serve.

M SAUSAGE & ROOT VEGETABLE SHEET PAN Take 8 good-quality pork sausages. (If they have been seasoned with sage and seem quite herby, reduce the quantity of fresh herbs listed in the main recipe.) Add the sausages to the hot baking sheet 10 minutes into the roasting time. Simply toss them in a little oil and dot them in between the vegetables. Remove a sausage from the baking sheet and cut it through the middle to test that it is hot and cooked through before serving.

MEXICAN TORTILLA WRAPS
WITH CHIPOTLE DRESSING VE

2 red and 2 orange (bell)
    peppers, deseeded and
    cut into strips
3 tablespoons olive oil
2 corn on the cob/
    ears of corn
400-g/14-oz. can
    black-eyed beans
2 ripe avocados,
    peeled and pitted
freshly squeezed juice
    of 1 lime
1 fresh red chilli/chile,
    deseeded and finely
    chopped
4 flour tortillas
large bunch of spring
    onions/scallions, sliced
small bunch of
    coriander/cilantro
sea salt and freshly ground
    black pepper
Vegan Cream, to serve
    (see page 8)

CHIPOTLE DRESSING
2 tablespoons chipotle paste
2 tablespoons olive oil
1 tablespoon red wine
    vinegar
2 teaspoons sugar

SERVES 4

Roasted peppers morph into the juiciest, sweetest delights and make a fantastic filling for these moreish tortilla wraps, especially when partnered with crunchy fresh corn, black-eyed beans and ripe avocado.

Preheat the oven to 190°C (375°F) Gas 5.

Scatter the (bell) peppers over a sheet pan, drizzle over the oil and roast for 15 minutes, until they are starting to soften and char.

Cut the kernels from the sweetcorn/corn cobs, add them to the pan with the pepper strips and cook for a further 10 minutes. Drain and rinse the beans, and add them to the pan to warm through for 4–5 minutes.

Meanwhile, mash the avocado flesh in a bowl and add the lime juice and chopped chilli/chile. Season to taste.

For the dressing, whisk the chipotle paste, oil, vinegar and sugar together and season to taste with salt and freshly ground black pepper.

Spread each of the tortillas with some of the avocado spread and pile with some of the bean mixture. Drizzle over some of the dressing, and scatter with a few chopped spring onions/scallions and some coriander/cilantro leaves. Roll up and serve with Vegan Cream (or regular sour cream for a vegetarian option).

M CHICKEN & BLACK BEAN WRAPS Prepare 2 chicken breasts following the Chicken & Tofu Hotpot variation on page 73. Shred the chicken into a bowl, season with lime juice, salt and pepper and add to the wrap filling. Substitute the Vegan Cream with sour cream.

STUFFED SQUASH WITH LEEKS, BLACK LENTILS & POMEGRANATE VE

Roasting the squash in its skin gives the whole vegetable such a fabulous texture and the skin is unbelievably good to eat. Serve with a rocket/arugula salad.

2 small butternut squash, halved and deseeded
4–5 tablespoons olive oil
handful of fresh thyme leaves
2 tablespoons freshly chopped rosemary
2 large leeks, trimmed and chopped
300 g/10½ oz. baby plum tomatoes
400-g/14-oz. can black beluga lentils
salt flakes and freshly ground black pepper

POMEGRANATE DRESSING
50 ml/3½ tablespoons olive oil
50 ml/3½ tablespoons pomegranate molasses

TO SERVE
50 g/scant ½ cup toasted pine nuts
3–4 tablespoons pomegranate seeds
rocket/arugula leaves

SERVES 4

Preheat the oven to 190°C (375°F) Gas 5.

Lightly score a diamond pattern into the flesh of the squash using a sharp knife. Drizzle with a little of the oil, sprinkle with the thyme and rosemary, place on a flat sheet pan and bake for 15 minutes. Remove the sheet pan from the oven and push the squash over to one side. Scatter the chopped leeks and whole baby plum tomatoes on the other side of the pan and drizzle with the remaining oil. Season with salt flakes and black pepper and return to the oven for a further 20 minutes, until the flesh of the squash is soft and the leeks and tomatoes are lightly charred.

Scoop the leeks and tomatoes into a large bowl. Drain and rinse the lentils, and add them to this bowl. Mix the olive oil and pomegranate molasses together and add about half to the lentil mixture. Pile the mixture into the squash hollows and return the sheet pan to the oven. Bake for 5 minutes, until the lentil filling is just heated through.

Remove from the oven, drizzle over the remaining pomegranate dressing, scatter with pine nuts and pomegranate seeds and add a good grinding of black pepper before serving.

V ROAST BUTTERNUT WITH BLACK LENTILS & GOAT'S CHEESE

Cut 200 g/7 oz. firm goat's cheese into pieces and fold into the lentil filling. Use this to stuff the squash and bake as main recipe. Sprinkle with extra goat's cheese along with the toasted pine nuts and drizzle with extra Pomegranate Dressing before serving.

MUSHROOM TOAD-IN-THE HOLE
WITH ONION GRAVY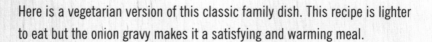

Here is a vegetarian version of this classic family dish. This recipe is lighter
to eat but the onion gravy makes it a satisfying and warming meal.

100 g/¾ cup plain/
all-purpose flour
2 eggs
60 ml/¼ cup ice-cold water
100 ml/⅓ cup whole milk
6 Portobello mushrooms
salt and ground white
pepper, to season
vegetable oil, to drizzle

GRAVY
4 onions, thinly sliced
50 g/3½ tablespoons butter
50 g/3½ tablespoons
plain/all-purpose flour
200 ml/1 scant cup whole
milk

*a 25 x 30-cm/10 x 12-inch
baking dish or 4 mini
baking dishes, lined
with baking parchment*

SERVES 4

To make the gravy, put the onions in a heavy-based saucepan with
the butter and a generous pinch of salt and cook over a low heat for
25–30 minutes, until they are just starting to turn a golden colour.
Cover the onions with the flour and continue to cook, turning the onions
constantly for a further 5 minutes. With the onions still on the heat, slowly
add the milk, stirring the mixture until all of the milk has been combined
into a thick gravy. Add some water if needed, to achieve the desired viscosity.

To make the batter, add the flour and a pinch of salt and pepper to a
bowl. Make a well in the middle of the flour and break both eggs into it.
Using a whisk, mix the eggs and flour together, starting slowly from the
centre. Once the ingredients are mixed, gradually add the water, mixing
to a thick paste. Finally, add the milk, whilst continually mixing with the
whisk until the batter is smooth. Cover and chill in the fridge for 20 minutes.

Preheat the oven to 180°C (350°F) Gas 4.

Drizzle the mushrooms with oil and sprinkle with a dusting of salt
and pepper. Place them, gill-side up, in the baking dish or dishes and
bake in the preheated oven for 15–20 minutes, until they are just starting
to turn golden.

Remove from the oven and turn the oven up to 200°C (400°F) Gas 6. Pour
the batter over the mushrooms and return to the oven for a further 15–20
minutes, until the batter has risen and is golden brown and crispy on top.

Remove the toad-in-the-hole from the baking dish or dishes and take
off the baking parchment. If whole, slice into four pieces and serve hot
with lashings of onion gravy.

M SAUSAGE TOAD-IN-THE-HOLE Omit the mushrooms. Prepare the batter as
main recipe. Take 8 plain pork sausages and put them in the roasting pan. Add 1 tablespoon
sunflower oil, toss the sausages in it to coat, then roast for 15 minutes in an oven preheated
to 200°C (400°F) Gas 6. Take the hot pan from the oven and quickly pour in the batter, then
bake for about 40 minutes, or until the batter is cooked through, well risen and crisp.

HARISSA-BAKED SQUASH
WITH AVOCADO & EGGS Ⓥ

The addition of spicy harissa to the already colourful flavour and texture combination of green avocado, bright orange butternut squash and eggs, is the ideal way to marry all of these ingredients together. It's rich and tangy in flavour, but the mellowness of the other ingredients contrasts well.

2 tablespoons harissa paste
2 tablespoons olive oil
550 g/1 lb 3 oz. butternut
    squash, peeled, deseeded
    and roughly chopped into
    2-cm/³⁄₄-inch cubes
1 ripe avocado, peeled,
    stoned/pitted and
    thinly sliced
freshly squeezed juice
    of 1 lemon
60 g/¹⁄₂ cup stoned/pitted
    black olives
15 cherry tomatoes
4 eggs
freshly ground
    black pepper

SERVES 2

Preheat the oven to 200°C (400°F) Gas 6.

Stir together the harissa paste and olive oil in a large bowl then toss in the butternut squash and stir again to coat the squash.

Put the butternut squash on a sheet pan with sides and bake in the preheated oven for 30 minutes.

Meanwhile, prepare the avocado and squeeze over the lemon juice to prevent it from turning brown. After 30 minutes, add the olives, tomatoes and avocado to the butternut squash and bake for a further 10 minutes.

Make four wells in the vegetables and crack in the eggs. Bake for another 6–9 minutes until the egg whites are cooked. Season with freshly ground black pepper and serve immediately.

──── ──── ──── ──── ──── ──── ──── ──── ──── ──── ──── ────

Ⓜ **BREAKFAST SHEET PAN WITH CHORIZO & EGGS** Omit the olives and add a 200–250-g/7–8 oz. package (about 10–12) of Spanish mini cooking chorizo. Add these to the baking sheet with the tomatoes and avocado. (If the chorizo you are using is particularly spicy, reduce the amount of harissa paste in the main recipe to 1 tablespoon.) Finish as main recipe.

──── ──── ──── ──── ──── ──── ──── ──── ──── ──── ──── ────

The Scrapbook of My Life App
(Coming in April 2016!)

SCAN
HERE

Hey guys!

I really **hope you enjoy** The Scrapbook of My Life, but I don't want this book to be all **about me!** So I've left the **odd page either** blank or partly filled so that you can grab a pen and get involved too, and save your memories for you to look back on in the future.

Those who **purchased my** other books (The Pointless Books) loved the integrated apps! So of course I had to have an app feature in **this** one too! Just look out for the scannable icons and point your device at them to reveal some never-before-seen content. Including some super-old footage of me as a little **kid** that I probably shouldn't have put out there for the world to see... but it's too late now!

You can also add your own photos to the memory booth and share them with me, your friends and the rest of #ThePointlessGang! Just don't forget that you need an Internet connection, so that you can download it and use it on your iPhone, iPad or other Android devices.

Enjoy guys!

Alfie x

5

THE SCRAPBOOK OF MY LIFE

You know that messy/dirty little diary you tuck away under your bed crammed with random ~~moou~~ moments of your life? That's kinda what this is for me! This little book you're ~~holding~~ is packed full of random little stories that have ~~happened~~ to me throughout my life so far.

I'm currently ~~21~~ 22 years old and looking back on my life so far... saying 'so far' sounds stupid. I'm only 22 haha! I'm half writing this for you to read and half for myself to look back on when I'm older and can laugh at all the things I've done in the past.

I don't really know where or how to begin... I'm not used to this writing thing at all! After all, I dropped English language about 5 years ago...

In fact, what I'll do is leave some spaces/pages empty so that you can fill out parts yourself to look back on in the future. It'll kinda be like a shared diary between you and I!

Right, since I still have no idea where to start, I guess my birth is the best place? I thought it'd be best for me to go visit my parents house and dig through the thousands of photos they've taken of me throughout the years. Annnnd also pick both their brains, as they remember EVERYTHING!

Ugh I just realised that I'm going to have to hand-scan in all the early photos of me as there was no such thing as a digital camera when i was a kid! haha

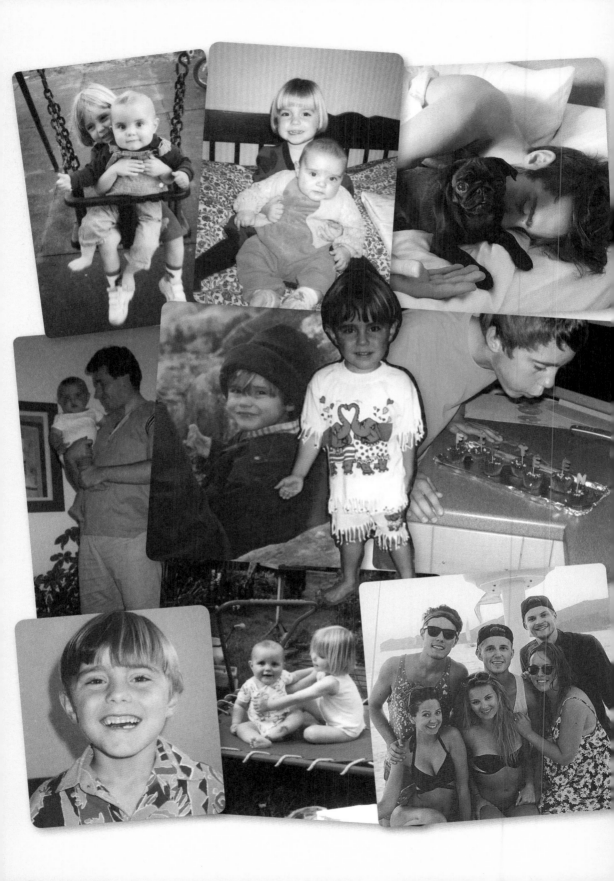

BABY STATS

20 minute birth

9.2lb

Caesarean birth

Asthma

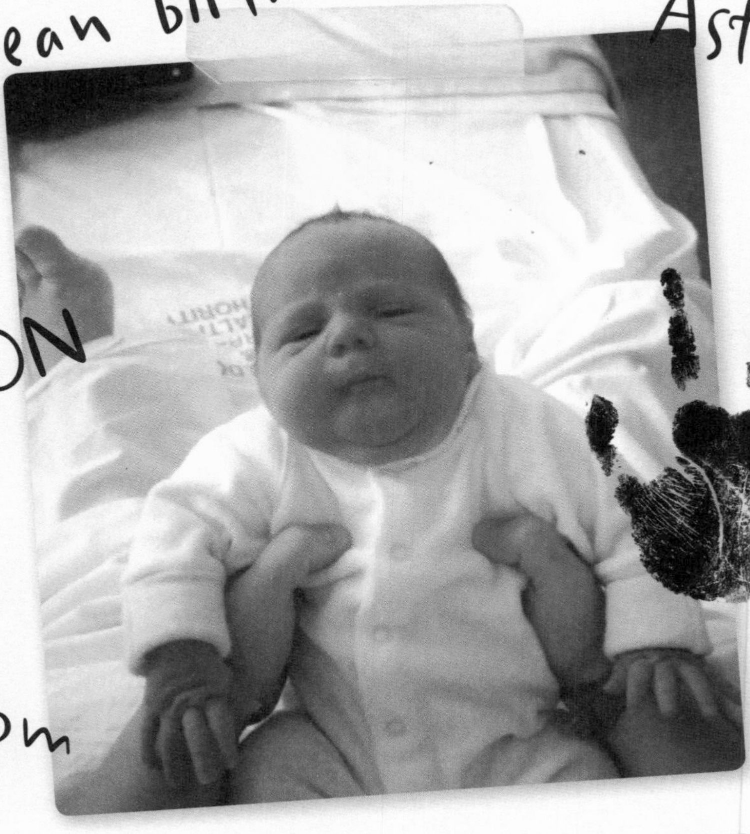

LONDON

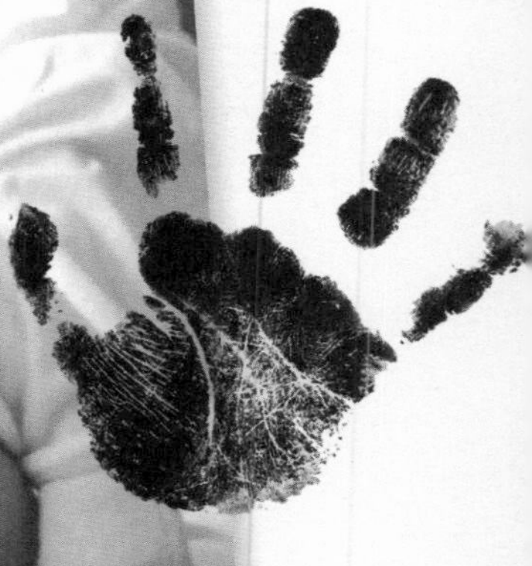

3:40pm

Cyst on my lung

17.09.1993

ALFRED SIDNEY DEYES

Shadow on my head

What about you?

10

Obviously I don't happen to remember being born so I can't exactly write the beginning of this book acting like it was yesterday. But what I do know is that being born is weird. Really weird. Me, I was pulled out of my mum's stomach... nice! I was a big baby at 9.2lb and I'm guessing that most of that was my head.

My sister has always told me the reason I was a caesarean birth was because my head ~~was~~ was so damn big... I kind of believe her!

Usually when you're born you're placed in your mother's arms right away, but for some reason they gave me to my dad and my mum didn't actually get to hold me for about 20 minutes.

The doctors and nurses then found out I had a cyst on my lung, which meant I was in and out of hospital **constantly. It eventually went away after 9 months!**

Basically I was a very easy baby... NOT!

oh yeah.. another little thing which made me really easy was having baby bronchiolitis for the first 2 ~~years~~ years of my life!

This literally meant I went non-stop in and out of hospital during this time period, ~~mean~~ resulting in many of my baby photos being taken in **hospital** ☺

13

HOW DiD I FORGET TO WRITE DOWN THE STORY EXPLAINING THE BLACK PATCH OF HAIR AT THE FRONT OF MY HEAD?!!

Right stick with me on this one as it's a pretty weird story that I myself don't quite believe, but my mum's friend is sure it happened.

So apparently if a pregnant woman asks you to do something for her and you forget or don't do it, it's bad luck? Yeah that's new to me too!

Anyways, when my mum was pregnant with me, my mum asked her friend if she could pick her up a Cornetto ice cream on her way back and you guessed it... she forgot! My mum's friend was sooo annoyed with herself and kept on saying she had to go back to the shop and buy one for my mum, otherwise her child (me) will be born with a mark somewhere on its body.

Annnd there we have it! I was born with a black patch of hair at the front of my head, which is still there until today! My mum calls it my Cornetto patch haha! This is literally the best example of why mothers know best. I'll never question anything my mum says, she's ALWAYS right!

15

THINGS I LOVED AS A BABY...

O Dressing up in anything, especially dresses...

O Following my older sister Poppy around
   everywhere. I was literally like her shadow!

O Sleeping with my finger in my dad's ear... Yeah
   I don't even know what to say about this one.
   I've just been told that it was apparently a thing.

O Having my toenails painted.

O Spot the dog!

   Climbing over/on/in every single piece
   of furniture in the house.

O My dad carrying me everywhere because I refused
   to walk.

                              here's your page

16

l in

LONDON

I was born in London and lived there until I was 3¾ (yep the ¾ is important when you're little) and the only thing I really remember is our amazing garden. My entire family lived within a 5 minute walk of our house, which meant my ~~⬛~~ aunts, uncles, grandparents and cousins were over all the time. I loved it! Our garden was pretty big and had a lot of things any child would love!

BRIGHTON

Moving to Brighton meant not only moving away from our family and friends, but changing nursery for me and school for my sister.

Only being 3¾ at the time, I ~~suppose~~ suppose I was a bit too young to realise what was actually going on, but for my parents it was a big deal! But I'm so glad they made that decision because Brighton is my favourite city in the entire world!

MY FAMILY TREE

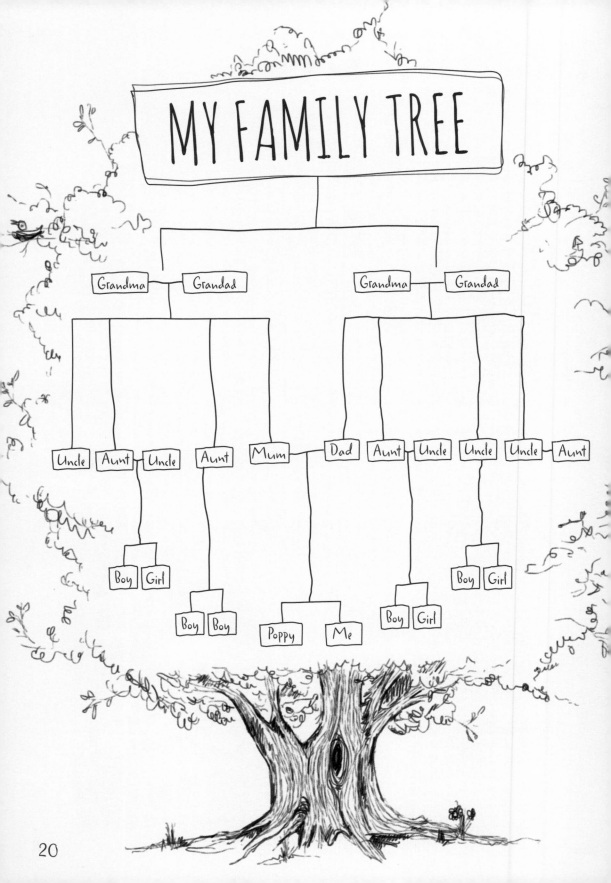

Grandma — Grandad   Grandma — Grandad

Uncle | Aunt | Uncle   Aunt   Mum — Dad   Aunt | Uncle   Uncle   Uncle | Aunt

Boy | Girl

Boy | Boy

Poppy | Me

Boy | Girl

Boy | Girl

your family tree

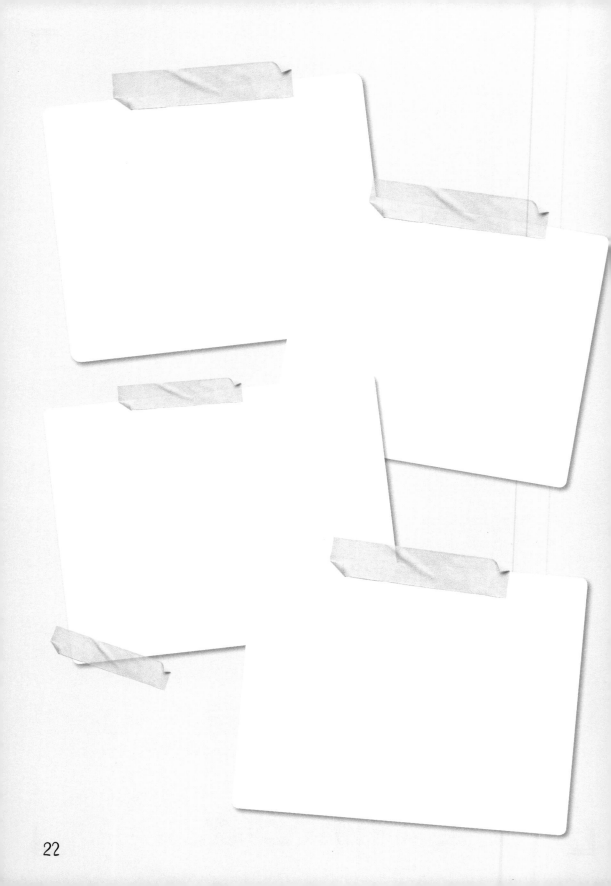

NURSERY WaS a LOT OF FUN

I mean, I swear it's impossible not to enjoy hanging out with all of your friends in one place AND having tons of different toys to play with! I loved playing in the sandpit with Morgan & Izzy, **my two nursery besties.**

I used to have speech impediment sessions every day because I **mispronounced** certain words, like instead of 'socks', I'd say 'docks'... nice one Alfie!! haha

MY NURSERY MEMORIES

I have so many memories of the time I spent at Balfour Infant school. I swear when you're little you just have no worries in your life... well, you do, but they're like 'Oh no I can't find the right piece of Lego to build my tower'.

To be popular in my class you had to either be good at skipping or cats-cradle and luckily I loved both of those things. I'd spend every break we had practising **with my friends. I mean, I was no expert,** but If I was asked to whip out a little **cross-over-armed-double-skip or the old Eiffel Tower** ~~cats-cradle~~, cats-cradle, I could do it haha!

One very vivid memory I have is a bit of a weird one... Let me start by telling you ~~from~~ the ending and then explain myself. I got caught in the

Nice bowl cut, thanks Mum!

reading corner just after punching a friend in the mouth and *knocking* her too**th out!**

Okay, okay so this is how it went:

My teacher was showing something to the class when one of my friends (can't remember her name... I was like 4 years old) asked me if I'd sneak off to the reading/book area with her. Now, to be fair, I thought this was just for a bit of fun! We managed to sneak off **without the teacher realising and once we were around the corner tucked** away, my friend **said** '**Alfie can you punch me in the mouth so my wobbly tooth will come ou**t?' Why, I'll never **quite know!** She could have just pulled it out like a normal person.

Anyways for some reason at the time I thought it was a damn fun idea and ~~then~~ punched her... INSTANTLY she began to cry and the teacher came running over to ask me what was going on..! Well, let's just say that was a tricky one to explain, as my friend sat there with her tooth in her hand, crying, with blood dripping out of her mouth.

27

School name

Teacher's name

🍴 Favourite school dinners

School play memory

MY MUM!

My mum's a super-creative person and always put so much time and **effort into activities for Poppy and I.** Everyday we'd be doing something new and fun like painting in the garden, decorating our clothes **or even building a stage for us to perform on!** Annnnd this stage has resulted **in multiple videos of me** dancing in dresses... I'm not **even going to try and explain myself. It is what it is!**

We used to love painting in the garden...

It was a few days before my friend Morgan's 4th birthday, so mum and I set out to buy him a present. We popped round to a little shop not far from our house that sold birthday decorations and little gifts for parties. After spending a good 10 minutes searching for the perfect present, the only thing I managed to find was a ~~funny~~ funny birthday card... but that wasn't really going to cut it haha! I couldn't NOT give him a present!

Whilst waiting for mum to pay for the card, I spotted it! The perfect present! Next to me, sitting ~~wibbobbobe~~ in a barrel full of soft toys, staring up at me was a little brown teddy. I popped it up on the counter. Morgan's birthday present was sorted!!... Well, at least I thought it was.

Mum was about to start wrapping up the teddy because if I attempted it myself... well, it would have looked like a four-year-old had wrapped it...

I remember taking the little floppy teddy out of the shopping bag and passing him to mum. And that's where it kinda went downhill. I mean, he was just too soft and cool... aannnd basically long story short... I kept **him hahaha! Which left Morgan yet** again with **no birthday** present!! So the following day we had to pop out and I ended **up buying him a pillow. What a great present Alfie...** a pillow!

He did have eyes but they've fallen out over the years...

To this day if Morgan ever comes over my house and happens to see Floppy, he tries to steal him back off of me

Write your favourite story about your friends...

STARTING "REAL" SCHOOL

After having so much fun at Balfour Infant School, it was time for me to move on up in the world and start year 3! I remember at the time feeling really odd about this. One ~~minute~~ minute you're one of the oldest children in your entire school, then literally a few weeks later, after the summer holidays, you start your new school and you're the youngest and smallest you can possibly be! Weird!

For some reason I have a few school memories that stick in my head more than any others... they're not even particularly amazing... well actually one of them is pretty cool so I'll tell you that one!

I was never a packed lunch kid, instead I preferred to eat hot meals for lunch which meant my parents gave me something like £1.80 each day to get a meal from the school canteen. Usually I'd be given a £1, a 50p and a few 10p coins or something, but I remember one day in particular my mum and dad left me a £2 for lunch. I spent the entire day playing with it in my pocket, flicking it up in the air, trying to guess which side it'd land on and rolling it across the table to and from each hand and then it happened! I kid you not, like this sounds stupid, but it's true!! The middle part separated from the coin, I'm not even joking! It split into the silver middle and the golden-coloured outside! I was obsessed! ...well kinda... until it came to lunchtime and I was so ~~hungry~~ hungry that I had no choice but to spend it on my school meal. Without sounding stupid, I've literally regretted it to this day!

SCAN HERE

ELIZABETH · II · D · G · REG · F·D · TWO POUNDS

Every single time I get a £2 I ALWAYS check to see if I can push the middle out ...and not once has it happened again!

MY FIRST PROPER HOBBY

I remember having to slip on my little black plimsoles, white T-shirt and shorts to play silly games in the school hall and somehow it counted as PE... we literally spent an hour throwing balls to each other and running around cones... why was that even a thing?

But gymnastics was different! I'd never taken part in any gymnastics before Mrs Caines began teaching my class. I mean I'd always loved running around and jumping off of ~~trees~~ things like walls and between my sofas (even though mum wasn't so keen), but never thought of taking gymnastics lessons. Well that was until I met Mrs Caines. I think she could just tell how much fun I had in her lessons and for some reason thought I was pretty good, so pushed me a lot harder than the other children in my class. If they were learning how to do a cartwheel, I was learning how to do a handstand.

It wasn't because I asked to do more difficult manoeuvres, Mrs Caines just encouraged me to do them. She believed in me and wanted me to succeed!

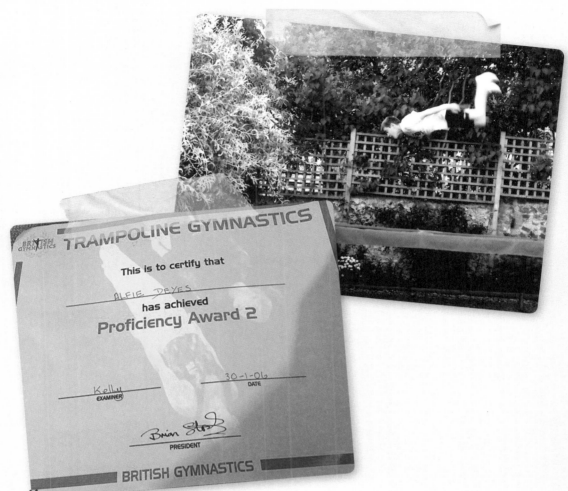

TRAMPOLINE GYMNASTICS

This is to certify that

ALFIE DEYES

has achieved

Proficiency Award 2

Kelly
EXAMINER

30-1-06
DATE

Brian St
PRESIDENT

BRITISH GYMNASTICS

I think Mrs Caines played an important part in who I am today. Although she may not realise this and might not even remember teaching me haha! Having her show me that if I put my mind to learning these basic moves, I could improve and learn things I never thought I could... I honestly think the courage and belief in myself she stamped on me has stuck with me to this very day and I'm so thankful for everything she taught me

Hahaa I DON'T EVEN KNOW WHERE TO start explaining this memory...

So I'll start again with what happened and then try my best to somehow explain why I did what I did!

I SHAVED MY DAD'S HEAD WHILST HE WAS SLEEPING!

I have no idea why I did it, I was too young at the time to remember... So what I'll do is explain what I think happened from what my parents have **told me over the years. My dad went to sleep just** like every other night and so did I. At some point during the night I got up (whether I was asleep or not while I did all of this no one will ever know), went into their bedroom, picked up his little beard trimmer and shaved a spiral shape into the back of his head without him waking up... I can't imagine my dad looked too great at work the next day with his suit on and new 'hair cut' haha!

I probably shouldn't have done this.

44

POPULAR CRAZES AT MY SCHOOL

I became OBSESSED with any craze! I couldn't just be average or okay at anything, I had to be amazing! Not to be better than anyone else, but to show myself that if I put the time into whatever it was, I could succeed!

This started out with Pokémon cards. I would beg my dad to buy me packs every weekend. I'd do extra jobs around the house to earn little bits of money to save up to buy packs. You name it, I'd do it. It was the unknown that I loved. The risk you took with spending hard-earned money hoping that you'd open the packet to find a rare card to take into school the next day. Then I discovered the Diablo... it took over my life. You didn't need money to get better, you just needed skill. For me, time = skill.

I would spend literally every second I wasn't in the classroom practising little tricks like over my leg, around my neck and the good old Chinese whip! (That was one of my best).

The Diablo became SO popular in my school, the teachers arranged for a local circus shop to come in one day and host a competition to find out who the best was from each year group (I was in year 5). I knew

I had a pretty good chance, but also knew that my friends Max and Asa were pretty good too.

After many tedious rounds of basic little tricks, I secured my place in the final 3... the final 3 being myself, Max and Asa haha! I can't quite remember how or why, but Asa went out next leaving myself and Max!!

The pressure was on! All those hours spent practising were about to be made worthwhile!

Out of nowhere Max suddenly drops his Diablo off the string, something that would send him out of the competition, but no... it bounces off of the assembly hall floor and lands back on his string...no one except me notices! Do I tell the judge what happened and place 1st, or keep it between myself and Max?!

I decided not to tell anyone and ended up placing 2nd with Max winning!! And from that day forward, Max and I have always joked about who's better and who should have actually won!

Next was the yo-yo, but I'm not even going to go into that one! I basically spent another bajillion hours learning random little tricks haha!

47

DO MORE OF WHAT makes YOU HAPPY

CHRISTMAS IS THE BEST TIME OF YEAR!

Everyone was happy, there was lots of delicious food and, little did I know, there were also TWO kittens coming! Poppy and I had sleepovers every Christmas Eve which usually meant me sleeping in Poppy's room on a mattress on the floor. My room was only about 10m away, but we always shared a room because it meant whoever woke up first could wake the other up and we'd both get to open our **presents earlier!**

After ~~the~~ running and dragging our heavy stockings into

Mum and Dad's room, jumping on their bed and making them both get out of bed, it was time to head downstairs and open our presents. I'm not sure what your Christmas traditions are like (if you celebrate Christmas) but we have always opened our stockings (from Santa) on Mum and Dad's bed... no earlier than 7am! And then we all meet downstairs in our pyjamas for some breakfast in the front room.

It happened whilst opening all of our presents to and from each other. Dad snuck off to another room to get one of Poppy's gifts... which was

50

odd since I **couldn't understand** why it wasn't under the tree with everyone else's presents. As Poppy opened the loosely **wrapped** box, two tiny little ginger kittens came bouncing out!! My sister, being the stroppy little girl she often was, started crying and ran upstairs because she 'didn't want kittens for Christmas'... What even?

Now, what I'm about to say sounds like some kind of film scene, but honestly it did happen!! Both the little kittens followed Poppy upstairs and sat outside the toilet door whilst Pop sat inside crying!

I think that was the moment Poppy fell in love with them and realised Todd and Tilly were the best **Christmas present ever!**

For ages the two kittens were called Todd and Tim, but after taking him to the vets we found out that Tim was in fact a girl and so **we chan** changed her name to Tilly! Toddler (Todd) and Tilly!!

My favourite time of year

SCAN HERE

Always DO
SOmething
Until You CAN
DO IT.

Don't Quit

CAMPING

Camping trips with my family were just the best! We used to FILL up the car with everything we could possibly want to take with us! Even double duvets instead of sleeping bags so that it was more comfortable. And the most fun bit of all was that it wasn't just our family, but our friends' families too! Every year we'd go in a big group of about 6 families... Having water fights during the day, going on long bike rides and making camp fires in the evening to roast marshmallows on!

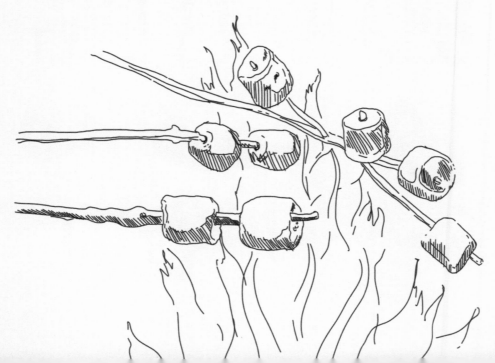

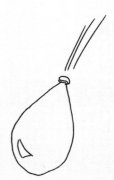

STARTING ANYTHING NEW IS SCARY...

Let alone separating from half of your friends to start an entirely new school with new subjects, new teachers and new pupils... buuut everyone has to do it!

Dressed in my new uniform and feeling like a grown up, I was soo excited to start secondary school and meet new people. I remember my first lesson with everyone sitting in their little groups of friends and not really talking to people they **didn't already know haha!**

Little did I know this very day I'd be meeting some of my best and oldest friends for the very **first time.**

I was that kid in your class who got dropped off and picked up by his mum everyday... Usually this would be embarrassing, but it meant I got to wake up 20 minutes later every morning! In fact, I'd even get my mum to **pick up my friends on the way so** they didn't have to walk either!

*If you haven't already gathered, my parents are **the best parents in the world***

I think it was also a tiny bit easier for me, as Poppy was three years above me in school so for the first two years of secondary school, I knew she was there if I ever needed anything. In one of the first few weeks my English teacher tried to give me a ~~20~~ 30 minute detention for not doing my homework. Buuuut I had a legit reason for it not getting done (I can't quite remember exactly what that reason was, but it was a good one... even if it was or wasn't true).

I remember saying I needed the toilet, calling Poppy up and asking her to come down to the English section and persuade my teacher not to give me a detention!! It worked haha!!

$$a^2 + b^2 = c^2$$

I always enjoyed school and always wanted to learn. I wouldn't say I was crazy smart, but If I was interested in a subject and wanted to do well I'd always get good marks. But when it came down to subjects that didn't really interest me, I'd always revise just enough to pass so that I could put the rest of my time into the subjects I enjoyed e.g. maths and science.

My family call me

'GOLDEN BOY'

I have no idea when this first started but it's stuck since such a young age. I'm guessing it's because I've always had a ~~neat~~ knack for talking my way out of things/getting away with stuff I should get told off for. It's kinda hard to explain haha! Basically if I were to get away with something and Poppy didn't, she'll say it's because I'm 'the golden child' or 'golden boy' and my parents' favourite. Whiiichhh obviously isn't true as no parent has a favourite child. But it's funny because so often I'll get away with doing something that Poppy would <u>never</u> get away with!

Over the years it's become more and more silly and and if I were to ever go for lunch with one of my parents or clothes shopping or anything where Poppy isn't with us, it's because I'm 'golden boy' haha!

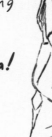

4TH PLACE... OUT OF 4!

I'd never had a gymnastics competition before so I didn't quite know what to expect. I had learnt my floor routine inside out and how to do one of those funny arm-up-in-the-air things that you have to do to the judges at the beginning of your routine. As Mum and I **watched people of other age groups take their turns, we realised that** I was the only person wearing a vest and shorts... literally no one else **except me! I looked at my coach, embarrassed...** Mum went to ask a member of staff if I could buy a ~~new~~ leotard at the venue and luckily for me, I could! I ran over to the little shop area and picked up a plain black leotard and popped it on. **SO MUCH BETTER!** I suddenly looked like I had a chance haha.

Every gym floor feels different, some can be more springy than others so I was a bit unsure of what to expect. I walked over to the centre of the floor, did the arm thingy followed by my routine (which actually went pretty well). **Next was my vault, which again can vary vastly due to the equipment used on the day,** but luckily for me it managed to go okay. They began to call out the names in order of positions from 4th — 1st, which started with mine! Meaning I came 4th!! I was happy with that, considering it was my very first competition!

Oh yeahhhh... I should probably let you know that in my group there were four of us.. HAHA! Buuuut 4th is 4th and that's all people who weren't there on the day needed to know ha!

Tons of training went by and it was time for the Sussex boys finals. This was a lot bigger, more prestigious and difficult than my original 4th placing competition.

The age group was 11-13 and I'd only just turned 11... not exactly fair considering all the other boys were either 12 or 13. Annnd the boy who'd won the two previous years in a row was 13 years old and up against me...! As we warmed up I kept myself to myself and didn't really speak to any of the other boys. They were all a lot louder – talking about previous wins and moves they'd learnt for their routines. Safe to say I was pooing my pants! I did my very best and just like last time everything seemed to go ~~really~~ pretty well. One of the straight-faced judges even cracked a little smirk! A few hours later, after watching the other groups do their part, it was time for the medal ceremony! Each category sat in a line and were called up in front of everyone, one at a time. 'Sussex boys 11-13 floor and vault'... I literally felt like staying sat down I was so nervous.

They started with 3rd place... my name wasn't called. The boy, who'd won both years previously, stood next to me, whispered in my ear 'I bet I've won again'. I looked at him in disbelief as they called HIS NAME out!! As it hit him and his face dropped I whispered back 'no you didn't haha'. At this point I didn't even care who'd won, I was just so happy that he didn't!

'ALFIE DEYES'

I looked around confused... wait huh! I'd won!! As I walked up and took my place on the highest podium I looked down and smirked at the boy stood next to me holding his silver medal! I'll never forget that moment!

THE TIME I SHAVED MY HAIR FOR CHARITY

My school was having a charity day where everyone could wear what they wanted if they donated 50p to charity. There were also lots of fun activities they could get involved in instead of lessons for small amounts of money (which also went to charity) e.g. throw a wet sponge at ~~the~~ the principal's head... play in a football tournament for the afternoon... or buy cupcakes from students who were having a cake sale. But, me being me, I thought I'd take it to the next level! So a few weeks before the charity day, I decided I'd shave my side-fringed-Justin-Bieber-style hair completely off and ask friends and family to donate money for me doing so!

The evening before the school charity day I went down to where I usually got my haircut and asked them to completely shave it off! I explained the reasons behind the bald head and my hairdresser agreed to do the cut for free as it was for a good cause. He said he'd start at the back of my head so that I couldn't see how short it was and if I did decide to change my mind, it would be too late as, by the time I'd see it, the entire back of my head would be hairless haha! I ~~remember~~ remember seeing **my mum's face...** **literally like this** Ö

I mean, I knew it was going to be short, but mannn it was SHORT! Literally bald!! I'd never seen my actual **head bald before** – it was sooo **weird. I remember getting home and crying** so much because I hated how I looked! I couldn't look in the mirror without wanting to go back in time. The only thing that kept me happy was knowing that I'd raised a lot **of money for young people between the ages of 11-18 who were terminally ill.** My first bald day at school was hard!

Sooo many of my friends had donated money to me for shaving my head and wanted to see what it looked like and the last thing I wanted to do was show people my bald head, which I was still not used to! I remember **wearing a hat as much as I could to hide my hairless** head. But thinking back to it, I shouldn't have been embarrassed at all! Not many young boys would completely shave their hair off to raise money for charity!

I'm soo glad I stuck with the idea and did it!

I'M NOT a CHEAT.

Well I'm not 'usually' a cheat.

What I mean is that I'm good at cheating and I never get caught... except this one time haha!

Monopoly has always been one of my favourite games! I think it's because it's silly and fun, but also a little bit strategic and I love coming up with strategies to solve problems. And in Monopoly terms, that's either not having enough money to buy something or trying to persuade another player to trade a card I need.

Well anyways, this time, let's just say money wasn't the issue... I had PLENTY of that! So, as per all Monopoly games, we played for hours and hours with people gradually becoming bankrupt and leaving the game to watch TV, play Snake on their phones or to grab snacks from the fridge. Now I honestly can't remember who won the game, but strangely that's not the important bit in this story.

I woke up the next day with a text from my friend Neil asking me to pop over as he had something to show me (this is the

66

boy whose house we played Monopoly at the previous night). Neil only lived on the road next to me, so later on in the day I ran over and letssss just say I wasn't expecting him to show me what he did!! Is recording **a friendly Monopoly game on a camcorder a normal thing? I suppose...** Neil's Dad had just bought a new camera and was playing around with it that evening.

With his entire family huddled around his computer screen, I pull up a chair **and sit-down. He clicks play...** I still have no idea what's happening **at this point!** Everyone around me starts to laugh as we all sit watching as I 'get up to go to the toilet' whilst playing the game, walk past the Banker (person **who looks after all of the money in the** game) and grab a wad of money whilst no one is watching...

I leave the room and return a few minutes later and continue playing as if nothing had happened.

I LITERALLY GOT CAUGHT STEALING MONOPOLY MONEY ON CAMERAAAA! Hahaa! I swear I don't always cheat, it was just that once...

RUNESCAPE AND HALO... TWO ONLINE GAMES THAT I PLAYED FOR SOOO MANY HOURS EACH AND EVERY DAY!

It sounds weird, but when playing these games it felt like I was in a zone. I can't quite describe it, but time would pass like crazy! I remember once my friend came over at lunchtime, us both grabbing snacks and sitting at my family computer to play RuneScape. Next thing I knew, my parents came upstairs and asked if my friend was staying over? We both turned and were like... huh? Why are you asking that, not realising it was 11pm! We literally hadn't stopped playing for 8 hours!! (My Mum's just read this page and said she wouldn't let me game this long but I definitely did!)

SCAN HERE

I'd spend entire weekends with 8-12 friends all crammed into one bedroom, each with our own Xbox and TV brought over by our parents early on a Friday night. We'd then spend all of Friday evening, all of Saturday and most of Sunday (until going home in the evening) playing Halo 2.

We'd all be running on literally a few hours sleep with our eyes STUCK to the screens. If anyone were to fall asleep, they'd for sure be pranked by everyone else, so I'd always make sure that I'd stay awake the entire time haha. And that took a LOT of fizzy drinks, pizzas and chocolate..!

I can't even describe how fun these weekends were! Hanging out with so many friends at once and gaming all day/all night.

69

START LIVING & doing Things you ENJOY

I was given pocket money for doing chores around the house... **well, t**hat was until I realised that I could earn the same amount of money much faster by doing easier/ more fun things than cleaning and hoovering or drying the dishes. This started off at a really y**oung age and gradually** became more and more apparent as I got older. I'd like to say **selling cards** outside my house was my very first job at the age of **around 7 or 8 haha!**

I used to fold a **piece of A4 paper from my parents'** printer and write 'Happy Birthday' on it. **Or if I was feeling particularly fancy,** I'd walk down the road and look out for a nice-looking flower, pick it and stick it to the front of the card. I'd then **take a small table and chair, and** place these outside the front of my house and wait for generous-looking people to walk past. These people weren't yet aware that they needed a card for a family member/friend, **but it didn't take much ~~persuasion~~ persuasion to make them part with 50p or £1** when a smiling child is asking them to purchase a handmade card haha!

I used to do a lot of little things like that and over the years they evolved and changed into other things, **such as** doing my **sister's chores if** she didn't want to do them so that I got double the pocket **money that week.**

And then came 'my' paper round...
One of the first jobs a lot of teenagers get in the UK is a paper round, which is basically delivering newspapers either early in the morning (**no chance I'd ever wake up that early**) or in the evening (my newspapers had to be delivered before 6pm). You have to **be 14 or older to** get a job as a paper boy/girl... but as usual I came up with a scheme to get the job **whilst being 13.**

I asked my friend's brother, **who was 16 at the time,** to **apply for the job** and then he let me pick up the papers each day and paid me the money at the end of each week! **I probably wouldn't do this if I** were you... thinking back to it he could have ~~more~~ easily taken a percentage of the money and never told me! I'm pretty **sure he didn't... and if he did, it serves me right haha!**

As you can tell by now, growing up **I always did what** I could to make money in the most beneficial way possible for me **and it kinda** didn't stop with my paper round! This is going to make me sound so lazy, **but I see it more as** finding a good solution to something I didn't want to do. And in this case, that was to go out in **the cold for 20** minutes every day (minus Sunday), delivering newspapers to houses (even though it was my job). **I knew my dad** liked going on early morning walks, so he used to deliver **my papers every Saturday** for me whilst walking to the local shop to buy a paper for himself **(thanks Dad!!)**. This left me with **Monday to Friday. Except it kinda didn't** because **the majority of the time I'd leave it so late on** purpose that my mum used to end up driving me around stopping at each door *whilst I* ran out of the car and popped the paper through the letterbox, jumped back in and repeated for the 37 houses I delivered to. **Looking back I don't know why Mum didn't just tell me to quit the job haha!** Mum and Dad collectively did the majority of the work!

This **happened** ~~unless~~ unless for some reason Mum couldn't **help me out and it wasn't a Saturday. In this case,** I worked out the quickest route, timed it on foot, skateboard, scooter and bike. **Turns out using a scooter was the** quickest, **so I used to be able to scooter the** entire round in just over 12 minutes... don't ask me how I remember that haha!

UGH I remember a few *times* having to deliver them in **the morning as I was busy after school and literally walking into** spiders webs outside every single front door! Then trying to get the web off of my face with my hand and rubbing newspaper ink all over my face... **great!!**

74

My worst/dream job...

You know what's the best? Spending time with your family! Growing up I used to go on holiday once a year to places like Greece, Turkey and Portugal. We'd stay in pretty basic accommodation, but this didn't matter because the best part of the holidays were spending time **with my family sunbathing, messing about in the sea and exploring.**

Back in 2005 to 2006 we stayed right on the beach in a little town clalled Yalicavak, Turkey for a week.
It was a super-friendly little town with a row of local shops and stalls around the corner, which Poppy and I would visit a few times a day buying random little things we'd never actually use like the metal drum I **bought myself** or the laser pen I BEGGED Mum and Dad to let me buy for days and days...haha! We never used them, buuut at the time they were amazing. We'd spend all day swimming in the pool/sea and running back and **forth from the little ice cream ~~shop~~ shop buying Magnums (my favourite ice cream).**

I remember buying a little fishing rod with Dad and walking around for ages to find a little jetty that we could fish off and we actually caught a fish! Not even joking! We enjoyed this holiday so much we went back the following two years!

My favourite holiday has been...

I'M NOT REALLY QUITE SURE HOW ANY OF THIS HAPPENED, OR WHY IT HAPPENED TO ME... BUT IT DID.

My school had a school council (a school council is a representative group of students who have been proposed and elected by their peers to represent their views and raise issues with the Senior Managers and Governors of their school.)
Yes I did just copy that down from Google...

Anyways! Thinking back, I'm not really sure how I ended up being in the school council, nor am I sure how I ended up being Vice Deputy Head of my house... but I was! In simple terms, it meant **I had to attend one meeting every few months and chat about ways we could improve certain things about the school** e.g. the uniform (I'll come to that one in a sec), litter issues and how the teachers can make the pupils more engaged in lesson time. My favourite part was that we got **to miss out on lessons for the meeting, and have tea and biscuits!**

Somehow my involvement in the school council lead to me being voted for the Vice Chair for South East of England's student council – which meant not representing my friends anymore, but representing the SOUTH EAST of England!! I'd occasionally get to miss a day of school and get driven to a super-posh school a few hours away to chat about what my school is doing to make it the best it possibly can be for its pupils. And yep — you guessed it — drink more tea or hot chocolate and eat more biscuits.

ALFIE DEYES
Vice Chair for South East of England's Student Council

I'm not going to bother sitting here and write much more about all of these weird school council opportunities/moments I had, but I just wanna jot down one more before I forget!! When I was in Year 10, my Head Teacher decided to move to a new school, which meant we needed to find a new one to replace him.

Now, usually this would be nothing to do with the pupils... but again like with all these other little stories, for some weird reason, I was involved. I spent the day interviewing possible Head Teachers and jotting down what I liked and didn't like about them; literally things like how friendly they were, how they sat, if they were too formal, if they were funny! I was one of five opinions in the final decision!! And, in case you were wondering, yep I did vote for the one who got picked in the end!

Ooh wait! Another ~~quick~~ quick story, as it's funny I promise!

Towards the end of Year 10, when the new Head Teacher started working at our school, he decided he wanted us to refresh the uniform and asked me what I thought it should be like. So I decided it should be a super-strict blazer and tie for Years 7-9 and then much more casual with a white T-shirt and black jeans for years 10-11... and they went for it!!!

I literally made it so my Year (10) and the Year I was about to go into didn't really have to wear uniform, but the rest of the school did and got away with it!!

Vice Captains

Alfie Deyes 11STM
Tilly Grivell 11STM

EVENINGS AFTER SCHOOL...

I'm not quite sure what it is about drama and acting that I love so much, I think it may be the buzz that you get once you walk off stage. Actually I think it's also about the friendships that you make with all the cast and crew putting on the show. You'd spend sooo many hours with the team each day and it feels kinda like your new family!

During school I was in three musicals:

Fiddler on the Roof

West Side Story

Jesus Christ Superstar

As soon as it hit 3:15pm, my friends and I would all head down to our local park (usually Blakers or Preston) and just hang out. Not in a dodgy-looking-teenage-mob way — we'd just relax in the sun, kick a football around, eat snacks and chat for hours and hours.

I've always had just as many female friends as male. I don't really understand the 'you can't be friends with a girl without fancying them' thing... I'd spend time with girls in the exact same way I would with boys. Being so close to Poppy while growing up probably influenced my respectful attitude towards girls.

IT WAS GREAT FUN BEING PART OF SOMETHING AFTER SCHOOL.

PLANNING & SETTING Goals IS key

NO ONE ELSE IN SCHOOL WATCHED YouTube LIKE MY FRIENDS AND ME...

We didn't visit the site to watch dogs riding skateboards or cats falling off walls... well, occasionally we did, but mostly we watched 'YouTubers' – people who uploaded videos frequently to their own little pages on the site. There weren't that many 'YouTubers' around at the time, so there wasn't much variety if you liked that kind of thing.

I think the reason I became so obsessed with watching these 'YouTubers' was because they were being themselves! They weren't acting, they weren't even reading a script; they were just chatting about topics that interested them or filming what they got up to that day. It felt like such a refreshing change from scripted TV shows with unrealistic storylines. But, more than that, you knew that the person you were watching behind the camera was just like you! A normal person! But they just happened to be on the other side of a computer screen.

My friends and I had always filmed stupid little videos when hanging out playing basketball, doing tricks on the trampoline and skateboarding. So instead of the videos being held on a memory stick, we began to put them on YouTube. We didn't aim to gain lots of views or subscribers; it was just somewhere we could put them so that we could all watch them whenever we liked.

After putting up a few of the most embarrassing skateboarding/parkour videos, I began to edit videos of myself playing video games (such as Halo 2 and 3, and Modern Warfare 2). I didn't have any experience in filming or editing, but since I was making the videos purely for fun, I also didn't have the pressure of having to create them in a certain way to get a good grade in an exam. So I suppose I just spent all my spare time after school learning how to film and edit the best I could... and to do this I watched sooo many editing tutorials on ~~YouTube~~ YouTube of course!

I remained obsessed with watching YouTubers, even while I made my own gaming videos! I begged my dad to take me to London to see CharlieIsSoCoolLike (one of the first YouTubers I became obsessed with) perform live. It was a ~~pretty~~ pretty weird thing to spend my time watching someone else sit in their room chatting about funny topics, so persuading my dad that it was a good idea to travel all the way to London to see him (and not even meet him) was pretty hard ha!

I managed to persuade Dad though, and after hours of queuing up in line I got to see CharlieIsSoCoolLike live and it was awesome! It was strange seeing someone in person, who I'd watched for so long every week, literally standing there in front of me!!

Going to this event made me even more obsessed with YouTube and made me want to start making videos of myself (even more) than I ever had before!

86

I remember sitting down and making my very first YouTube video like it was yesterday. Balancing the family camera on a stack of Xbox games and DVDs (adjusting the stack a little so the camera was at head height), I pressed the record button without knowing what I was going to talk about or **how I was even going to introduce myself...**

'Hello! Hey! Hey guys! Helloooo, how're you doing? Hello, my name's Alfie!'

It literally took me about 1,000 takes JUST to say hello to the camera! Not to mention ~~how~~ how quietly I was speaking

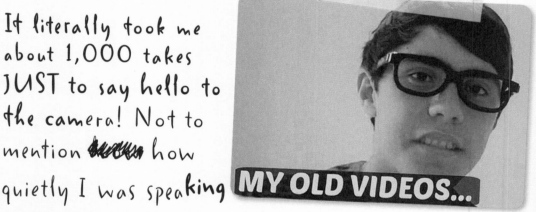
MY OLD VIDEOS...

since I didn't want my family to overhear me talking to myself (the camera). I didn't want ANYONE to know what I was doing.

You have to remember that vlogging wasn't a normal thing! No one was even watching vlogs back then, let alone creating them... what the heck would people think if they knew what I was doing?!?!
I did my best to make sure no one found out. I decided to create an account on YouTube under a name

none of my friends would ever be able to link back to me. It took me ages to think of one — until I thought... what kind of videos am I actually going to make? Is anyone going to bother watching them? Doing this is literally pointless... and that was it!! Pointless! And what was I creating?! Video blogs...

And at that very moment

POINTLESSBLOG

was born hahaha!!

The reason I decided to create my own YouTube channel on that particular day was because I was bored bored bored!

The rain was pouring down outside and I couldn't get out of the house. So what did I make my very first video on?? 'What To Do On A Rainy Day!' Hahaa! The only thing I actually remember from this video (luckily, because it was sooo embarrassing I wouldn't want to remember any more details) was that I played Monopoly against myself... yep one of my ideas of what to do on a rainy day was to literally play Monopoly ALONE... great video Alfie!

SCAN HERE

IT WAS SO STRANGE... I LITERALLY DIDN'T KNOW WHAT TO DO OR SAY!

Six of us decided to go to the cinema (can't quite remember what we went to see), but as we left something happened that will stick with me for the rest of my life (remember at this point my friends didn't know I made videos).

As we were walking out of my local Odeon cinema I heard someone behind me say 'Alfie?'... I turned around expecting to see a friend or family member... but no one I knew was there. 'It's Alfie, right? I watch your videos, man.'

... SOMEONE RECOGNISED ME FROM MY YOUTUBE VIDEOS!!

I had 1,600 people subscribed to my YouTube channel, but never did I think someone in the street – someone I didn't know – would actually care enough about my videos to stop ME and ask for a photo!!

But this wasn't the only thing rushing through my head!! My friends... my friends didn't know I made YouTube videos!? What do I say to them? How do I explain this? I don't even fully know what's going on... it doesn't feel real and now I have to try and explain the situation.

I was so overwhelmed with everything going on. I spent around 20 minutes chatting to the three boys who stopped to say hello, as well as let them help me explain to my friends what I was doing. I'm not going to lie: having people stop me in the street because they watch my videos was a pretty damn good way for my friends to find out what I'd been up to in my spare time!

COLLEGE YEARS

Leaving Varndean School to start at Varndean College was a real step forward into reality! Not only was I leaving somewhere I'd attended each and every day of my life for the past 5 years, but I was also leaving behind so many amazing teachers and friends.

I knew I'd still see them often, but it wasn't going to be the same as sitting with all my friends in one room every day. But I ~~although~~ guess that's part of growing up! Learning to physically move away from people and still keep the friendship as strong as before is tricky, but so valuable.

Picking subjects to study **is strange because you have so many** different people giving you their opinion on why they think you should be picking a certain subject, but you **know what really matters? What YOU want to do!**

The reason you're picking these subjects to study is because you might want **to continue learning/ working in that field** in the future.

Choose the subjects you love not the ones
you <u>think</u> you should be learning!

I'VE always BEEN VERY LUCKY iN THE RESPECT THaT I HaVEN'T REaLLY *FOUND* *MaKiNG NEW FRiENDS TOO DiFFiCULT.*

I've always surrounded myself with people similar to me and as soon as I arrived at college, I did that straight away.

One thing that was pretty weird when starting college was having a different timetable to the usual 8:45am – 3:15pm that I was used to at school. Some days I'd be working at college from 8:45am – 4:30pm and others I wouldn't even have a lesson that day! And on others I'd be in at lunchtime and finish **after just** two hours or so. Should I even write about revising? I found it SO difficult to concentrate by myself and revise. Like sooo difficult!

I remember one time I even spent £250 on noise-cancelling headphones JUST so I couldn't hear anyone else in the college library and get distracted and talk to them... Yeah, you guessed it... they didn't stop me! I mean, I'd spend hours each day in the college library attempting to revise, but would just end up chatting to my friends...

Just a bit of advice: **REVISE! REVISE! REVISE!** There's no point studying a subject if you're not going to work hard to get the best grade possible! The only person you're letting down is yourself...

Revision Notes

CONVINCING MY PARENTS WAS THE HARDEST THING!

I was going to write 'hours and hours', but that just wouldn't be true! So lets **start with** 'months and months'...

...Months and months were spent persuading my parents that allowing me to buy a Vespa motorbike would somehow be a good and responsible idea! Yes I know they are dangerous, etc.

But I've always been a sensible person and... well, actually, why am I telling you why I should have one? haha!

I finally managed to persuade my parents into agreeing that it would be an 'okay' idea, not a 'good' one, but they approved enough for me to go ahead and purchase one for myself!

I'd saved up enough money from working and found the perfect one online. Being able to drive where I wanted when I wanted gave me so much freedom!

It also allowed me to set my alarm later each morning because driving to college and work on my Vespa took literally 3 minutes! I'm sure my mum ended up loving it too! It meant she no longer had to drop me at my friends' houses, etc.

I WAS THE ONLY ONE WHO THOUGHT THIS WAS a GOOD iDEa...

The only job I've ever had (I don't count my paper round, as my parents did most of it hahaa) was working part-time in a retail shop. And when I say 'part-time'... I literally mean around 4-8 hours a week, maybe 12 if I was lucky! I was paid lower than

the minimum wage, but to be honest I wasn't even that bothered because I used to have so much fun working. I'd mess about with the other staff so much, try on all the clothes and make my own work outfits from the shopping bags...

So not only was I going to college every day, and working a part time job, but I was also spending hours every day creating my little videos for YouTube! Whiiiicchhh kinda meant I had no time left to revise...

I had been made part of what was called the 'YouTuber Partnership Program', which allowed YouTubers to have advertisements at the beginning of their videos and earn a tiny amount of money every time someone watched one. I was only getting a couple of thousand views per video, so it never really amounted to much... But one particular month was different. I remember the moment so vividly like *it was yesterday!*

I received my monthly email telling me how much money I'd made from YouTube on the same day as my weekend job sent me a letter in the post *telling me how much I'd made from* working there. It turns out my YouTube videos had earned me over £2 MORE than my actual real life job haha!

A normal person would see this situation as: AMAZING! NOW I GET TO EARN DOUBLE as MUCH as I WAS PREVIOUSLY EARNING WHEN WORKING JUST MY WEEKEND JOB!

Then, of course, there's how I read it:

AMAZING! NOW I'M **EARNING** MORE FROM YOUTUBE, I CAN QUIT MY WEEKEND JOB AND SPEND ALL MY TIME JUST MAKING VIDEOS!

Annnnnd that's what I did! Despite EVERYONE around me telling me that quitting my weekend job was a stupid decision... I went in the very next day and handed my notice in!

I'VE always BEEN CONFiDENT iN WHaT I DO.

I think one of the most important things in life is to be comfortable and confident in your own skin. It sounds so simple, but I honestly don't think I know many people who are completely comfortable within themselves.

If you want something, go **and get it!** If you want to change something, go and change it!

I'll always put my time into things I love doing. You can see this from me putting more time into creating YouTube videos than I did into revising for subjects I didn't enjoy at school! Or me quitting work as soon as YouTube paid me slightly more!

Most of all you've got to believe in yourself! Believe that what you're doing is right and WILL work out. Not might, not hopefully... it WILL!

the ONLY Moment you REALLY HAVE is RIGHT NOW, SO MAKE THE MOST OF it

SCAN HERE

YOU KNOW WHAT'S WEIRD? THINKING THAT, BEFORE YOUTUBE, I DIDN'T HAVE SOME OF THE AMAZING FRIENDS I DO TODAY.

As my audience grew on YouTube, I began to speak to other people who made YouTube videos more and more. I remember speaking to Marcus Butler when we both had less than 300 subscribers!

I was amazed that someone who lived so close to me also made YouTube videos. Chatting via DMs on Twitter we agreed to meet up and shoot a few videos together — which was weird because I'd never filmed with ANY friends before and now I was agreeing to film with someone I'd **never even met or spoken to in person...**

In fact the first time Marcus asked me where I lived I answered 'Lewes', which is a little town about 15 minutes away from where I actually lived. I didn't want him to turn out to be a creep and know where I lived haha! Annnd then when we came to actually ~~film~~ film together, I had to **explain why** I wasn't travelling from Lewes and in fact I only lived 5 minutes away from him!

It was strange. Within no time I went from hanging out with other YouTubers purely to make videos and do live shows together to going shopping, to the cinema and out for dinner.

SCAN HERE

These people were no longer 'YouTube friends' but just normal friends of mine that I happened to meet from creating videos. It was also so refreshing being able to properly speak about video ideas, views and getting recognised with people who fully understood exactly where I was coming from.

As you can probably guess by now I didn't exactly put all my time into getting the best grades at college. In fact, I was so caught up in creating YouTube videos, going to meetings about my YouTube videos and helping YouTube create new features on the site, that my college teachers told me that if I had work I needed to get done for YouTube, I could miss my lessons!!

I was literally told by my teachers that I could make YouTube videos instead of attending lessons and they would understand!

Of course I still went to the vast majority of them and worked hard whilst at college, but if I neeeeeded to film something for a company I was working with, or had an important meeting during the day, I had the option to miss the occasional lesson.

It kinda made me feel that everyone was wanting me to succeed and do well with this little YouTube thing I spent so many hours each day doing!

I don't know why I'm writing this really, but it's just a funny little story that I'd like to write down so that I don't forget it in the future.

How to create Youtube videos

GETTING TO KNOW ZOE

Zoe and I **had been** speaking for 2 or 3 months via Skype and texting etc, but since we lived three and a half hours away from each other, it's not like we could pop out to spend time together. Oh yeah and the fact that I couldn't drive — that would have been **helpful!**

It was the 17th September (my 19th birthday), my family had all gone to work and as usual I was Skyping Zoe, telling her about **the presents my family had given me.**

Suddenly I heard a knock at the door, but I wasn't expecting anyone to be coming over... Zoe started laughing as I jumped off my bed and walked downstairs to see who it was. I opened the door to see a pizza deliveryman standing in front of me. He passed me a **massive box, smiled and walked away... Instantly I knew Zoe was up to something** haha! I ran upstairs, jumped back on the bed and showed Zoe the box and saw her little face smiling back! 'Happy Birthday **Alfie!'** she said. I opened the box to *see my favourite pizza* — tuna and sweet corn (I know its a weird mix, but it's so so delicious).

Anyyywayysss as I said I'm purely writing this down so that I don't forget this **little story in the future!**

YESTERDAY WILL always BE in the PAST & TOMORROW WILL always BE the FUTURE

RaNDOM FaCTS:

- I've never tried a cigarette

- I've never tried ANY drugs

- I was born with a weird patch of black hair at the front of my head

- I get obsessed with things super-easy

- I've only ever been in two relationships

- I spend ALL of my time making YouTube videos

- I'm super-close with my family

Here's one thing I don't want
to forget in the future...

HERE'S SOME LIFE ADVICE:

If you ever get asked to go bungee jumping say NO!

So Marcus and I were asked if we wanted to go bungee jumping — no wait, that's not even true!
Marcus was meant to be the one doing the jumping and I was just in the video with him, but not jumping myself (so glad I wasn't asked... I would have been way too scared).

So we arrived at the highest bungee jump in the UK and I spend the first 10 minutes laughing my head off at Marcus because he was so scared! We sat down in a little tent chatting to the instructors about safety regulations when out of nowhere one of the camera crew turns to me and says 'oh yeah... I forgot to tell you that we booked you in to jump as well. Wait a second... what?! The team has booked ME in to jump without even asking or telling me! There was no chance, literally NO CHANCE I was to risk my life and jump off!

Well, that was until I saw a group of six teenage girls all giggling away to one another about how much 'fun' it was... Yep they'd just done the jump! They were sooo young, yet not scared at all! So I had to do it.

Immediately after seeing the girls, I signed all the forms with Marcus, had our harness put on us and before I knew it, I was walking up THE scariest stairs I've ever seen in my life... I'm not even joking, I thought I was going to die. **They were** so wobbly and the higher up we got, the more the wind t**hrew us around.**

I remember saying to Marcus... why are we even doing this? It's not fun at all. I feel like I'm about to jump to my death, man!

Marcus went first and swan dived perfectly over the edge! Next it was my turn. I stood up and hobbled over to the edge (my feet were strapped together and the bungee rope was attached to my ankles). As I got closer and closer, a man standing on the edge said to me 'don't look down, just ~~████~~ KEEP looking straight ahead...'

I instantly looked down.

Why I didn't listen to him, I'll never know...

You see, jumping off something is easy. Blocking out the fact that you're about to jump off one of the tallest bungee jumps in the UK and hoping your bungee cable doesn't break and that you don't just just splat on the floor below... that's the hard bit! It's ALL mental.

I threw myself over the edge annnnnd I don't really remember much else apart from spinning and spinning and spinning as I was dangling over the water below me, before waiting for the little boat to drive over and lower me down back to the ground.

As soon as I landed the two men on the boat were cheering and jumping up and down...

'NICE FLIP MAN!'

'YOU SHOULD HAVE TOLD US YOU WERE GOING TO FRONT FLIP!'

Sorry, what...? I did a front flip? Haha!

Turns out I dived off of the edge and, as I was falling, I performed a front flip! I used to perform flips and somersaults all the time when I did gymnastics, so I guess I instinctively performed a flip in the air. Not that I remember...

To be honest, it didn't even look cool! I looked like a floppy mess falling off a bridge! And that's why I'm writing this: to tell you that there's simply no fun or enjoyment in bungee jumping and don't ever bother doing it, hahaha!

FIRST BIG YOUTUBE MEET UP

I can't really describe what meeting those who watch my YouTube videos is like. I suppose the only way to describe it would be like making a friend online and then finally meeting that person in real life! Whenever people stop me to say hello in the street, they're so happy and full of energy. No matter what kind of mood you're in, it's impossible not to smile and get excited, and because of this a few friends and I thought we'd hold a meet up where viewers could meet us in person.

We promoted the event over social media, but never really knew if people would actually turn up, or care enough to travel to see us...

But as we walked towards the meeting point in the park, we could see soooo many people!! It was crazy – actually MAD! As we got closer and closer the screams were intense and everyone started running towards us! I couldn't believe what was going on. Little me who makes silly videos in my bedroom now had hundreds of people here just to see me, how crazy is that!?

We spent hours and hours hanging out, taking pictures and filming videos and although there were a LOT of people, everyone was so supportive, friendly and relaxed (after the initial few minutes haha). It felt like we were hanging out with loads and loads of friends at once. No one was more important than anyone else and the atmosphere was just so friendly and fun! It was amazing to spend time with everyone and say thank you for watching our videos.

There were more people than this

I'll never forget the feeling I felt when walking towards the park expecting to see 10, maybe 15 people, and then out of nowhere seeing the excited faces of hundreds and hundreds of people! This was for sure one of the first moments where I felt purely overwhelmed and shocked by the little online community I'd created!

NOT SUCH A GOOD DAY FOR ME...

As you know I'm not great at revising, so you can imagine AS Level results day was never going to be a great day for me, haha! I write 'haha' because I literally spent half of the day laughing — I didn't really know what else to do! When I'm nervous I often laugh... even when I'm in a situation where I really shouldn't be laughing!

My friend Holly and I walked up to receive our results together. Both of us knew we weren't going to have the best results and were already regretting wasting so much time not revising! We said to one another that whatever results we received, we wouldn't judge each other and wouldn't be sad if we didn't get the grades we wanted.

3, 2, 1 OPEN...my hands froze and I literally couldn't open the envelope! I wanted to open them somewhere with just us so that no one else was there to ask me what grades I received.

You know that annoying thing that ALWAYS happens when someone REALLY smart from your class comes up to you and says 'so what result did you get?'

And I say, 'Errmm a "B"'

And they say, 'No way, congrats! That's so, so good.'

'Oh thanks! **What** did you get?'

And they say, '...Ohh, **not great, I only** got an "A" but wanted an "A*"'

DON'T EVER BE THAT PERSON!

Anyways, Holly and I decided to go to the school library. We sat down and opened our results together... and I'm going to be honest, I really didn't do too great! Buuuut it was all my fault — I spent all my spare time watching/creating YouTube videos so what else was I ~~expecting~~ expecting?!

Holly and I walked back to my house and decided to just watch a film and give ourselves some time for our results to sink in, hoping that it'd kick our butts into revising more in the future...

I'VE always BEEN TORN BETWEEN LIKING AND DISLIKING THE SOUND OF GOING TO UNIVERSITY.

I love learning about topics that interest me, but am not so keen on the whole exam system, and how if you wrote one extra sentence in an exam, it could change the outcome of your entire grade, and even your future career. Surely there's a better way to measure skill and intelligence?! And let's not lie: people only learn stuff to pass the exam and then forget half of the things they learnt after taking the test!

Before my exams

after my exams

My parents are both academic, with my dad studying at Oxford purely for fun and then going to another top university afterwards. My ~~dear~~ sister Poppy studied fine art at uni and scored a first in most of her exams, so I had a lot to live up to haha! I'd always joked that I was the smarter child... but here I was spending ALL my time creating videos for YouTube whilst Poppy was doing sooo well at uni!

I've always been incredibly lucky to have such supportive parents who have always let me take my own path and do what I love. I'm sure they would have wanted me to go to university and get a degree, but at the same time they could see how much fun I was having creating videos, and could see that it was my passion.

So yeah. Unless I was going to uni to make new friends and learn new life skills, I wasn't really into the idea. However, just in case I changed my mind, I applied to a top media university in London. It was something completely different to anything I'd ever studied before (Maths and Science), but I thought, as I enjoyed making YouTube videos so much, I'd rather spend three years at uni learning more about that kind of thing.

WHAT I'M ABOUT TO SAY COULDN'T SUM UP MY LIFE ANY MORE IF I TRIED!!

After traveling for two hours, I arrived at Ravensbourne University in London for my interview. It was weirdly empty; I first thought maybe everyone was sat in a separate waiting room before their own interview? Or that maybe I was the last person of the day?

I walked over to the check-in desk and presented the woman with my interview form. She looked confused and said 'Erm, the interviews were ~~actually~~ actually yesterday' and pointed to the date at the top of my OWN printed out piece of paper! Yep I'd literally turned up the day after all the interviews! Typical Alfie!

She asked me to go take a seat whilst she called up stairs to see if the man who was holding all of the interviews happened to be in to have a chat with me... I felt like such an idiot! What a great first impression! Turning up on the wrong day!

Somehow the man holding the interviews happened to be in and was even free to have an interview with me in his office! Phew! I jumped in the lift and went up to his office to meet him. You know what's even funnier? When applying for a creative subject at university, you're asked to bring your portfolio of work, including work from previous media classes you'd taken at college or school. I'd kinda never done any media lessons before, so I took my laptop and some of my YouTube videos with me haha!

We chatted about YouTube, the future of TV/ the Internet and why I like making videos, for about 20 minutes. I remember, just as the interview was coming to an end, he said 'One last question Alfie. What do you feel is going to be the next big thing in the technology world?' or something along those lines. And I answered: I think 3D TVs will become normal and people will be able to have them in their own houses, not just at the cinema. (Fast forward to now and I have two 3D TVs in my house! I was right!).

I honestly couldn't believe what happened next! Right there and then, I was offered a position at the university! He literally said 'Although I'm not actually allowed to tell you this as it's only *the interview*, I'd like to offer you a place at Ravensbourne University because the aim of the course is to get you out there into the world of media and you're already out there doing that.'

TYPICAL ALFIE:

TURN UP ON THE WRONG DAY FOR MY INTERVIEW.

SOMEHOW **MANAGE** TO GET AN INTERVIEW.

GET OFFERED A PLACE AT THE UNIVERSITY THERE AND THEN!

I don't know how I get away with this stuff!

My final A-level exams were just a few weeks away and I still hadn't started revising. YouTube was taking up **all of my** spare time and I didn't want to give it up because I **was having sooo much** fun doing it and it was actually **starting to go** somewhere! Whilst all my friends had their heads tucked into books, I had my head in front of my laptop screen...

I ended up revising for *1 hour* per exam... I had 10 exams and only did 10 hours of revision.

NEVER DO THIS!!

I honestly **sat in some of my** exams asking myself why I didn't revise more, but there was nothing I could do! It was too late to *realise* that!

You know what I hate? When you come out of a Maths or Science exam and ask your friends what they wrote for one of the questions, hoping they'd reply with what you answered! Then they say something different to me but similar to each other. That's when I knew I'd messed up.

RESULTS DAY.

For sure one of the scariest moments of my life! I felt so sick!

To receive my A level results, all I had to do was log into the college ~~car~~ system from home any time after 7am and **my results would be waiting there** for me, along with the result of my university application.

I sat down with my family, nervously logged into the college system and clicked through to see if I'd been accepted into University or not...All that was running through my head was 'Alfie why didn't you revise more?! Buuuuut it was too late to worry about that — there was nothing that could change my results now!

'CONGRATULATIONS'

Wait, sorry, what?!?... I'd somehow been accepted into university!! But I hadn't revised? I found my exams sooo hard? What? When? How? Hahaa!!

I was sooo confused — surely I hadn't fluked all my exams and somehow got the grades I needed to get into uni? That's literally impossible!

I scrolled further down to reveal my A-level results for each subject (Maths, Chemistry and Geography). Something was wrong — something was weird! I scrolled back up and refreshed the page.

'CONGRATULATIONS'

But I hadn't scored high enough results to get into my university course... Yet it still said I had been accepted? Grabbing my mobile, I gave the university a call, because I didn't want to celebrate if there was some kind of mistake! **And that's when yet another one of those weird moments happened to me, when I get incredibly lucky...** It was right, I HAD been accepted! But what the heck, I didn't get good enough A-level results?

After speaking to the woman on the phone for a good 10 minutes, she told me I'd impressed the leader of the course (the man who interviewed me) so much that he gave me an unconditional offer!! Whatttttt!? That basically meant that whatever A level results I got, I was guaranteed a place on the course because the university wanted ME on the course!!

I WAS **ACCEPTED INTO UNIV**ERSITY WITHOUT HAVING TO REVISE!!

... this definitely isn't a photo of me wearing my sister's graduation gown.

MALFIE BREAKING RECORDS

Ever since I can remember I've been obsessed with the Guinness World Records books, receiving the newest one every year from my mum and dad. If you were to visit my parents' house, you'd see the books all lined up in order, starting in 1996 (I think).

The reason I like *the book* so much is because it's about being the best in the world! If you get your name in the book, it means no one else is better than you at that given thing! Wait... since we don't have proof that aliens exist, technically if you have a Guinness world record, you're the best in the universe! How cool is that!?!
Out of all 7 billion people, no one can do that thing better than YOU!

Since reading my first copy of the book I've always told my parents that I'll be in there one day! Of course it'd be for something stupid and weird, but I'd be in there one day! Growing up I'd practice all my weird little talents like solving a Rubik's cube or dice stacking, just in case it was my calling and I'd somehow make the book!

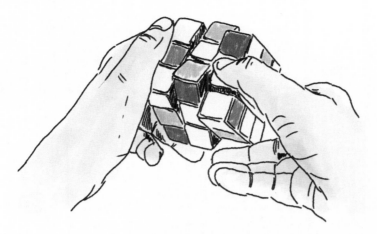

SCAN
HERE

Well, fast forward to 2012, Marcus and I received an email asking if we'd be interested in presenting a new YouTube channel for Guinness World Records!! Each week we'd be attempting to break a different funny world record on camera.

This was my chance to be in the book!!

Marcus and I had never filmed with a proper camera crew or even in a studio! For these videos we had our own paramedics in case something went wrong, along with our own make up artists, lighting team, audio man, camera team with three different cameras running at all times, and a Guinness official watching over us! Basically it was a LOT different to anything

Guinness World Records
SLATE:
100
MARCUS BUTLER
ALFIE DEYES

we'd ever done before, but it was exciting and something for us to learn and try out! But best of all we'd be learning it all together and having fun at the same time.

We filmed for a good two weeks but still didn't break any records! If it was just Marcus and I it would have been funny, but obviously it was all being filmed!! I can't even describe how much Marcus, the team and myself wanted to actually break a record!

Occasionally we'd have guests on for an episode to give them a chance to break a record (which was also unsuccessful haha). FunForLouis was on set and we were attempting to break a record for most party poppers popped in 30 seconds. Marcus went first, but unfortunately didn't make it; next was Louis, who also didn't make the cut and lastly, it was my turn to try and break the record. Considering we'd spent the whole day filming – in fact the whole week – filming record attempts, the pressure was on! And then, out of nowhere, I only went and beat it, popping 29 poppers in half a minute!! Hahaa yes it wasn't the most impressive record, BUT it was a record!! An official Guinness world record! I was going to be in the next book and in my mind that was enough to make childhood Alfie proud!

Over the next few weeks Marcus and I broke soooo many funny records! A few times I'd attempt a record first, break it and then Marcus would go next and beat my just-made record, instantly taking it away from me!

I think, overall, I had/have (not sure how many of ours have been beaten since we attempted them) nine records and Marcus has/had ten!

I was so excited to attempt to break all of those records on YouTube. But looking back on it, the most valuable thing I gained wasn't the records themselves, but the opportunity to hang out with Marcus for 6 weeks and spend more time with a friend.

And then also gaining the experience of working with a big camera team and getting used to filming high production videos!

What records do you want to break?

I WaS SOOO BUSY DURING THE SUMMER AFTER COLLEGE, MaKING YOUTUBE VIDEOS AND FLYING AROUND THE PLACE TO VARIOUS DIFFERENT MEET UPS!

I was still 'living' at home with my parents, although I was basically living out of a suitcase due to traveling so much and doing **YouTube videos.** I tried my best to spend every moment back home with either friends or family, to make sure **that my relationships back in Brighton** weren't affected due to YouTube. I'd literally film all day in London, get back to Brighton late in the evening, go out for dinner/ clubbing with friends and **then head back to do more** filming early the next morning.

Friends and family have always been super-important to me. I'm the friend who will call you at 10pm and say 'let's go do something fun!!' and you'll probably be in bed asleep haha! The amount of times I persuaded friends to get out of bed and com out for a late dinner/to go clubbing that summer was mad. It was the only way I could really spend proper time **with friends back home,** since I was mostly out of Brighton working on YouTube videos.

A midnight McDonald's with my friend Holly was always a good shout! We'd rock up in pyjamas and eat soo much food it'd put us to sleep haha!

SUMMER was amazing!

The freedom of being able to make YouTube videos as my full time 'job' was unreal. I inserted the marks around 'job' because I still don't really count it as my real job. It's more like a hobby of mine that I'm fortunate enough to earn enough money from. It's basically the same as it being just a hobby, except I don't have to go to work during the day and instead I can spend all my time working on new videos and projects!

Anyywayyyss summer was so good! It really opened up my eyes and showed me that maybe these videos could be my actual full-time job for a while. So I took a big step and decided to defer university for a year! Which basically means 'Thank you for offering me a place, but I'm going to have a year out of education and I'll come to university next year'.

Most people would take this time to grab a big rucksack, stuff it with important things and travel the world hoping to learn life lessons and to 'find themselves'... and then there's me! I took a year out to spend more time

working on making videos and hanging out with friends haha! Don't get me wrong, I was technically 'working' ~~maybe~~ because YouTube was my job, but I didn't see it like that! I saw it as a year with no lessons, to have fun and hang out with friends!

I'D rather SPEND MY TIME BUILDING my OWN Dreams than SPENDING MY Time Building Someone ELSE'S

THIS WAS PROBABLY ONE OF THE BIGGEST DECISIONS OF MY LIFE SO FAR!

My mum is one of those mums who loves to do everything for you. She actually enjoys looking after me and helping me with things like washing my clothes or dropping me off at friends' houses. So the idea of leaving home to live by myself was kinda **scary!** I literally had no idea how to cook, clean and pay bills! Basically everything you need to be **able to** do when living by yourself haha!

So instead of going solo I decided it would be a better idea to live with someone who's in the exact same position as me and also knows **absolutely nothing** about living by themselves...

So I decided to move in with Caspar Lee! Caspar was living in South Africa at the time, but we had met a few

138

times before through making **YouTube videos** together with friends.

So he flew over to London, jumped on a train to Brighton **annndd** we **kinda just decided on everything then and there once he was here haha!** It sounds like I'm exaggerating and it was more planned than this, but it honestly wasn't!

He arrived in Brighton and planned to live with my parents for as long as it took us to find a flat to move in together! A few days after Caspar arrived, we jumped on a train up to London **and booked in a few flat viewings.** The second place we went to see was perfect! We made an offer and agreed to move in **the NEXT day!!**

Everything was going so perfectly!! Soon we'd be living together, **making videos all day every day annnd** be in London! (Which if you don't know, is only 55 minutes away from Brighton so I could easily visit friends and family **anytime I wanted**).

Now...we had to somehow survive without our parents – **which was something neither of us knew how to do** – and we more or less ended up living on stir-fries, **takeaways and pasta for the first few months,** because that's all **we knew how to cook** (or at least **I know how!**)

I'M SAT HERE LAUGHING WHILST WRITING THIS!

I remember one time I was at the Sugg family house when Zoe received a FaceTime call from Caspar. (Sorry to Caspar in advance for embarrassing you haha! But it really sums up our time living together!)

Caspar called Zoe to ask her how to make pasta. Not even a pasta sauce; literally plain pasta! Like pasta from a packet!! He didn't know whether to use boiled water, cold water and heat it, or just cold water!

We were useless! We didn't even know how to wash our clothes. Of course we had a washing machine, we just didn't know how to use it. Wait actually I tried once! I washed 4 pairs of jeans and they all came out tiny and shriveled... so every time I used to visit my parents back in Brighton, I'd take a massive suitcase full of dirty clothes and my mum'd wash and iron them for me... this was at the age of 20! My mum's the best mum in the world! haha! But it really sums up our time living together!

142

There were loads of things Caspar and
I got up to – too many to write down
here... wait, one last one **haha!**
I remember one time we thought it'd
be a good idea for us to both join a gym and
start working out together each morning. We searched
online and found a local gym a five-minute jog away.
A few **days later we bought new** gym clothes,
jogged down to the gym and both bought *three-month*
memberships. **Yeahhh that was kinda the only time**
I went and I think Caspar went once without me...
what a waste! haha!

SCAN HERE

I DiDN'T HaVE a CLUE WHaT TO EXPECT!

After creating YouTube videos for a few years and occasionally attending the odd meet and greet, a group of us (Zoe, Marcus, Tanya, Jim, Louise and Caspar) decided it was about time to properly get out there and meet those who watch what we do. We'd already met a bunch of viewers who lived in the UK at various events and YouTube meets and greets, so I thought it'd be a good idea to travel ~~around~~ abroad this time! We never really knew what to expect – yes people watch our videos, but paying money and traveling to meet us in person is completely different! Would anyone actually bother coming to see us?

We all **had a very large audience in America** so we thought it was only right to fly over there for the tour and whilst we were so close to Canada, we added it into the tour too!

Each venue was between 2,000 **and 3,000 seats,** which thinking about it now, was crazy! They sold tickets out in minutes. Literally minutes! It was so, so mad!

00:00:43

We all sat down and started to plan what we were going to do on stage to make the show engaging and fun, but at the same time similar to our videos. It took days and days to plan our hour-long stage show; we had to make sure it would be good enough to perform in front of so many people at once! I can't quite remember who came up with the idea, but along the way we decided it'd be a good idea to bring special guests along to each of our shows to surprise the audience and bring a different element e.g singers/dancers etc!

It was all planned and ready to go and all that was left was to wait for the date to actually come about, and for us seven friends to fly across the world and officially be on tour!! A YouTube Tour!!

TIME TO FLY across THE WORLD WITH MY
FRIENDS AND BEGIN OUR TOUR!

TOUR - car MOBBED - FLiGHTS
EVERY MORNING - FANS EVERYWHERE

SCAN HERE

I LOVE TRYING NEW THINGS,

but when you've got a few million eyes watching your every move, it's kinda hard to 'try' something because if you fail, well, it's not the best haha!

So me being me, and putting more work on myself, I decided to start a gaming channel on YouTube! Not the typical games like Halo, which I played loads while growing up, but more funny and stupid games. Such as showing my embarrassing dancing skills on Just Dance or failing at Minecraft, where I'd record myself playing the game on my camera and at the same time record the screen of my game so everyone watching the video could see what was going on. Then I'd edit the two together so you can see the game and my reaction to me playing it.

Gaming was and still is SO popular on YouTube, so I knew there was an audience that might be interested in these gaming videos of mine, but wasn't sure if the audience that watched my vlogs would be interested in them.

...And then I started playing Sims with Zoe!

Growing up I'd always played hours and hours and hours of Sims with Poppy. We had every single expansion pack in a row next to our family computer! And back then, I swear there were like **15 expansions or something!**

Anyways, I thought Sims would be a good game to play on my new gaming channel, since it's kind of like daily vlogging, but talking instead about your fake family haha! The people watching my videos could help me decide what to build in the game and which jobs to give the characters — it was a joint effort. Zoe, who loved the game growing up, would sit and play with me too. Annnd let's just say it went **down well** haha! Each little video of Zoe sitting on my lap (as I only had one office chair) playing Sims would hit millions and millions of views!!

SOME OF THE BEST THINGS IN LIFE COME AT THE MOST RANDOM OF TIMES!

For example once, when a few of us YouTubers were having dinner, Marcus, Joe and I were sitting at one end of the table singing this song non-stop... agh I can't remember which one! But it was an old classic. Literally the entire meal we were crying, laughing and singing it together. After we'd all finished up eating and were sitting around the table chatting, we somehow came up with the idea of how funny it would be if we made a parody style boy band called 'The YouTube Boyband'.

Marcus, Jim, Joe and I headed up to Marcus' hotel room, balanced his camera and tripod on a little side table so it was **tall enough for us to stand** up and dance in front of... and that's where it all began.

150

There was no plan; we hit the record button and freestyled everything. Well I say that, but from the shockingly bad/funny video, it's pretty damn obvious that none of us knew what we were doing. We were ~~singing~~ singing and dancing for literally an hour, non-stop. Oh and I should point out it was like 3am, I have no idea how we didn't get kicked out of the hotel that night!

And for some reason, when Marcus put the video up online that weekend, people went **CRAZY!**

My comments and tweets online for the next few months were FULL of people asking for more boy band videos or photos.

What the heck had we started? haha!

I HAD SO MUCH FUN LIVING IN LONDON WITH CASPAR FOR EIGHT MONTHS OR SO, BUT IT ALSO SHOWED ME THAT LONDON LIFE WASN'T REALLY FOR ME.

I was used to living in a city where everyone knew each other and in a place where I **could** see family and friends in a matter of minutes if I wanted.

Whereas London was so busy, I'd literally wake up tired! I wouldn't have even done anything except walk to a cafe to grab breakfast and I'd feel tired from the amount of people everywhere.

Caspar also wanted to have a break from London and go back to South Africa for a few months, get some sun and see his family.

So we decided to hand in our notice to our landlord and enjoy the last few months of living together before he flew back to South Africa and I moved back to Brighton.

Back on the south coast, I moved into a flat on my own, which was weird because although Caspar wasn't any good at household chores, being alone meant I didn't even have someone who I could ask to see if I was washing my clothes right or whether I was using the right dishwasher tablets haha.

The main thing I enjoyed about living alone was the silence. That makes me sound so boring and weird, but there's something I find relaxing about my own company. I could do what I wanted when I wanted — such as walk around with no clothes on or dance to really loud music because it wouldn't wake up or affect anyone else. It was just me!

YOU KNOW *THAT WEIRD BOYBAND THING WE DID as a JOKE IN THAT HOTEL* ROOM FOR MARCUS' YOUTUBE CHANNEL? WELL THINGS WERE **aBOUT TO STEP UP a LEVEL.**

A few months after filming our stupid hotel room singing video, we received a call from Richard Curtis and Emma Freud asking us to pop over to their **house for dinner and discuss an exciting** project. Of course we all said we'd love to, in fact Zoe and Tanya also came along, we all hung out, played with their family cat a lot (it's the cutest thing ever) and eventually, after stuffing our faces with **food and cake**, got **talking about this project!**

*As you can **tell from** what you've read of this book so far, I'm not the best at writing, so I'm not going to try and explain the entire evening to you... so I'll summarise the outcome *

We (The YouTube BoyBand) were asked to record a song with a music video and **everything to raise money for Sport Relief!!** The song and video would be professionally recorded in London and would go live on YouTube for everyone to see!

One **slight** issue... could any of us actually sing?

Appreciate every MINUTE of EVERY DAY AS YOU never KNOW what TOMORROW BRINGS

RECORDING OUR VERY FIRST SONG...

Turning up, we had literally no idea what to expect. As we walked into the recording studio, we were told that a number of different artists had recorded massive songs in the exact same place.

I couldn't help but hope that someone had warned the recording team that we weren't actually singers and we were simply doing it for charity.

All the boys squished up together on one little sofa next to the sound engineer's table... or I'm guessing it was something like that haha. It had so many buttons on it I swear it would be nearly impossible for one person to even know what they all do!

We started running through the song with each of us singing our parts out loud, just to warm up and let the sound team know who was singing which parts etc.

And then it was time... I, for sure, did not want to embarrass myself by going first! ...Wait, have I actually mentioned how bad I am at singing? Yeah let's just say pretty damn awful! Watching the boys sing their lines in the little 'audio booth room' (I'm just making up all these terms as they sound right haha) it was my turn.

I did my part and tried to just have as much fun as possible by remembering the reason I was there, not to sound good, but to raise awareness and money for Sport Relief.

The hardest bit for me was not knowing what any of the other boys sounded like. The sound man kept playing parts back and saying things like 'go just a little lower/higher on that note' etc.

But not knowing **how low/high/good I** was scared me and I'd have to wait a few days until we shot the **music video to listen to the final mix of** the song.

157

The song had been recorded/mixed together and was ready for the YouTube boyband to hear for the very first time!

As we walked into this massive studio, it kinda hit me how awesome this music video and song was actually going to be! The very first thing I saw as I entered was a MASSIVE and I mean **massive** – like taller than my house – camera crane! The crew was setting up the cameras and sorting out the different video sets. We all went straight to hair and make-up (yeah boys get make-up too when doing video shoots haha!) and the woman doing my make up got a little electronic razor out, turned it on and said 'do you mind leaning forward for me?'

Wait, sorry, what? I was so confused and asked her what she was about to do.

'Bring your hair line at the back up a bit' was her reply. If you don't know already, I'm sooo fussy about my hair and there was no way I could let someone who I'd never met before cut my hair!! So I stuck with my hair being styled instead of cut haha!

I'm glad the team producing the video knew we were there to mess about and create a fun music video for a jokey song we'd recorded, because literally, as soon as we walked in, we all started being stupid. Thinking about it, it was kinda their fault for buying sooo many funny props to use. We were riding little tricycles and tandem bikes around the place, and wearing swimming clothes whilst getting our make-up done...

SCAN HERE

In fact, Caspar spent most of the day wearing a massive faux fur coat with a giant silver chain! Let's just say we didn't exactly take the day too seriously!

We were there to have fun and create an amazing video!

Filming was going super-well: we kicked it off with all of us on stalls, sitting in a line like a proper old-school boyband music video, pretending to play different instruments. I think one of us, maybe Caspar, didn't have an instrument, so was just playing the air guitar haha!

Then we changed into some white suits... we all looked ridiculous and were laughing at how stupid each of us looked! I looked like a really bad Elvis impersonator with a few buttons undone and my collar up. We filmed all the typical camera-above-the-boyband shots, with each person taking their turn singing their lines towards the camera.

We wanted to make the video as funny and stupid as possible, since it was for charity. So we were all doing stupid things on camera and just messing about having as much fun as we could.

There was actually a lot of footage that people never properly saw. We shot this underwater scene for sooo long, pretending to swim in tiny little shorts with inflatables and flippers haha! But when the video was all edited together, I don't think any of it, or maybe only a tiny part actually made the cut. I know some of the footage is out there in the outtakes or behind the scenes, but it's funny looking back on bits like that. When shooting big videos you sometimes spend sooo long on a scene and then it never actually ends up anywhere! But I guess that's just part of it.

Anyways, we wrapped up the shoot and were all so, so excited to see the outcome. It was weird having to wait to see the music video, because with **our videos we can turn an average** edit around in an afternoon. But for this I think we waited a few weeks!

I remember *being sent the* download link to watch the video for the very first time. I was SO nervous. What if I didn't like it? *What if people thought* we were **actually trying to do** a proper cover and sound/look good haha?

After watching literally 10 seconds of the video, I was obsessed! It was sooo us. **So stupid, jokey and fun! Annnd,** most of all, it raised awareness and money for an amazing cause.

I REMEMBER RECEIVING a RANDOM PHONE CALL FROM MY MANAGER ASKING ME IF I'D BE INTERESTED IN MEETING WITH a BOOK PUBLISHER WITH a VIEW TO WRITING a BOOK.

As anyone who knows me will know, I dropped English in school as soon as I could, so writing a book wasn't exactly something I'd ever thought about or wanted to do before. So I politely declined the offer for a meeting with the publisher.

A few weeks later I got another call from the publisher, who asked to meet with me to chat through different book styles and ideas. Again I wasn't interested in writing a novel or anything because writing isn't really for me. I like creating videos!

They called back and said it doesn't have to be a novel — it could be anything I wanted it to be. I couldn't really say no to that haha! So I agreed to meet them, but made sure they knew it wasn't likely anything was going to come from us meeting up.

Myself, my manager and two members of the publishing team sat down in a tiny, tiny little meeting room and chatted through different possible ideas — none of which were remotely close to a novel!

That's when we came up with the idea of creating something similar to my YouTube videos — including lots of silly challenges and things for the readers to do themselves, just like when people recreate videos I'd made at home.

I also wanted it to be something similar to the daily vlog style videos that I created. These were like time capsules for me to look back on in the future and to see what I was thinking each day and what I liked/didn't like at the time. And since the idea for this book was for people to fill it out, they would be able to look back at it in years to come and the book itself would almost be like a time capsule of their life.

I was so excited! No other YouTubers had really done a book before and the fact that it was an extension to the videos I made, I knew (hoped haha) that the people who watched my videos, would also enjoy the book! But obviously I was nervous! I'd never asked my viewers to pay for something before. Everything I'd done was for free, so I'm not going to lie, I was pretty damn nervous to see how people were going to react.

THIS BOOK CONSUMED PRETTY MUCH THE NEXT FEW MONTHS OF MY LIFE!

Even when I was away traveling with friends, I'd be bugging them all to help me come up with ideas for each page haha!

A load of us UK YouTubers flew out to Italy for a meet up/ YouTube event in Milan. It was super-exciting because although we had held meet-and-greets in the UK and America, we had never really held one anywhere else in Europe. No matter how many times I meet viewers, the amount of people who turn up and support they give is always, always, always overwhelming!

We were in Milan for three days, but that wasn't the end for the boys, we'd planned an epic road trip before going back to the UK. The girls all flew home, while the boys (me, Marcus, Joe, Caspar, Trove, Connor, Tyler and Louis) grabbed two cars for the week and set off to hit as many amazing landmarks as pos- sible in five days before flying back from Naples (over 500 miles).

I can't even describe how nice it was to relax with so many friends at once. The long drives **from city to city were probably** my favourite **part** of the trip. I love a **deep chat with friends and trust me** we had a **good few of those!** **We only had one place booked for the** night and booked the rest of our accommodation as we drove around each day. We got to see so many incredible things — an insane winery, the Leaning Tower of Pisa, the Roman Colosseum and so much more.

Whilst we got up to all these fun things, I was planning/writing my book, and as I was surrounded by so many creative people the entire trip, **some of the pages you've seen in THE POINTLESS BOOK** for sure came from some of the boys. So thanks for some of the ideas, guys! I remember sitting in this little **hotel, which was a bit** like a villa. Anyway we were sat in the lobby and it was raining sooo much outside that instead of going out and exploring, we decided to all sit in the lobby for few hours and have laptop club. That lobby was the place I emailed over the very first **draft copy of book 1!**

WHILST DRIVING AROUND ITALY, WE DIDN'T REALLY HAVE A PLAN.

We had a few things we knew we wanted to see such as Pisa and Rome, and we wanted to find somewhere to get a massage. All of us (except Joe) love to get a good massage and whenever we're traveling try and get one.

We'd heard about a crazy new winery that had just been built.

Thinking about it, I don't think any of us were even big wine drinkers, but we'd seen and heard about how amazing this place was and we had no time restrictions, so drove on over.

The people working there must have thought we were right weirdos! I can imagine their usual customers are 30+ year olds who take wine very seriously and here we were... a group of 20-something year olds all filming each other and joking around.

I'm not going to lie, it was actually super-interesting! We had a member of staff show us around and explain how the wine is made etc. After the tour we headed over to the on-site **restaurant where lunch had been set up for us for free!** (Major perk of making YouTube videos!)

SCAN HERE

We tried tons of different wines whilst eating and all bought a couple of bottles on the way out.

It was such a random, but fun day with the boys! And I'll never forget it — **since then I've loved red wine!**

IT WAS TIME FOR A CHANGE.

Something new. Something challenging but rewarding. It was time to start daily vlogging!

I'd had my second YouTube channel 'PointlessBlogVlogs' for quite some time and uploaded the occasional daily log style video. I loved filming the videos but not every day of my life was fun enough to film haha!

The thing I love about daily vlogging is how the audience can properly engage with someone everyday and trust me, once you start watching someone's life, it's so addictive! So with that in mind, I thought it was about time I challenged myself to film every single day for one whole month! It doesn't sound like much, but it's not just the filming and editing, it's keeping each video entertaining enough so that people want to watch you every day!

Anyways, it was coming towards the end of one of the most fun and productive months of my life and I sat back and thought to myself... why am I stopping? The videos were storing so many great memories, plus they're great fun to put together and my viewers are loving them — why should I stop!?

So I didn't. That would have been stupid!

As I sit here writing this very sentence, I'm still, to this day, vlogging on a daily basis!

'I'M THE SMARTER SIBLING!' I always JOINED WITH POPPY GROWING UP, BUT FOR SURE THIS WASN'T TRUE!

Whilst I was **having** fun creating YouTube videos **and traveling** the world to meet people who watched me, Poppy was living in London working her butt off studying fine art at university.

I always felt bad because I was constantly having fun with friends and whenever I spoke to Poppy she was working, working, **working.**

I had to keep on reminding myself that although she had to study really hard at university, **she also** was what that she loved!

It came down to results day and, **of course, she went and** smashed a 1st!

Since then I kinda don't mention the 'I'm the smarter sibling' thing anymore haha! I only just passed college and she's getting the best grades possible at uni!

THIS STORY IS ALL ABOUT PROBABLY THE CRAZIEST DAY OF MY LIFE SO FAR...

Waking up like any other day, I ate breakfast with Zoe whilst watching YouTube videos. Zoe had a taxi booked to take her off to a work day in London and I had a book signing that lunchtime, also in London! Originally I was thinking of jumping on a train and then either a taxi or tube, but since Zoe was already heading into London, I decided it would be stupid not to jump in her taxi with her...

This was my very first book signing and I had absolutely no idea how things were going to go... or if people were even going to turn up to get their book signed! I mean, I'd mentioned it in two or ~~two~~ three daily vlogs, but since it wasn't a ticketed event, I couldn't actually tell how many people were planning on attending.

About 30 minutes into the journey and still about three or four hours away from my book signing was planned to start, my phone started ringing. It wasn't good news...I was asked to delete all my tweets about the book signing and instead tweet a message asking people to NOT come along to the signing. At this point I should point out how difficult it was for my book publishers to even get me a signing in central London!

No book stores believed that I'd be able to get people to turn up to meet me and get their books signed since I wasn't a 'traditionally known celebrity'...
In fact I'm not any kind of celeb; I just make little videos that quite a few people watch for some reason!
Anyways, as my taxi turned the corner... things went pretty wrong! It wasn't just the 1,000s of people surrounding the cars outside the book store — screaming, crying and banging on the windows so hard that we thought the windows were going to break... but also the two HELICOPTERS circling above, making sure the crowds weren't getting out of control. Ohhh and the 15 policemen on horseback and countless police on foot... Yeeeahhh let's just say a few people came to get a book signed by me!

Zoe and I had literally no idea what to do. We both sat there looking at each other helpless. We were so, so, so overwhelmed. I'd never felt something quite like this before. Zoe burst into tears and I was sooo close to crying.

Not because we were scared, but purely because seeing so many people who were there to show their support for me and my new book! It was madness, like actually so amazing.

After the police helped me out of the taxi and escorted me into the building through literally a crowd of 8,500 people, I met up with my book publishers and management and we didn't even know what to say or what to think/feel. All I could think about was why did ALL these people come out of their way — get trains, drive and even fly from other countries — juuuust to meet me. I mean, yeah, I'd gone to YouTube events before with loads of other vloggers, but people weren't attending them just to see me! This was different. Those who were outside the shop were here purely to meet me and get their books signed!

I only managed to meet around 500 people before a commanding officer of London's Metropolitan Police came running in and requested to speak to me. At this point there were hundreds of fans standing in queues in front of me... I had no idea what he was going to say and with sooo many people watching and recording me, I couldn't stop thinking the worst haha!

I mean obviously I knew I'd done nothing wrong because I never ever expected over 8,500 people to turn up, buuuuut at the same time, they were all outside and it was crazy out there! He was super-calm, but said if he didn't get me out of the building in the next 20 minutes the shop windows and doors were going to be smashed in by my fans trying to meet me!

Sorry what?! People were legit trying to BREAK through the doors and windows to get to ME!

I carried on signing for as long as I possibly could (until the police told me I HAD to get out) after which I was driven off to a hotel on the other side of London where my friends and family were waiting with drinks and food to celebrate the launch of my book!

Not going to lie, I'll never forget that day! When talking about it, it feels like I'm exaggerating or lying, but honestly! It was mad...

SCAN HERE

BEING THROWN IN THE DEEP END.

That's exactly how I felt when my first book went to #1 on the bestsellers chart. Every TV show, radio station, newspaper and **magazine** wanted to interview me. How was **this kid who made little YouTube videos in his bedroom** suddenly breaking the book charts haha! To be honest I **had no clue myself!** All I **k**new was that those who watched my videos were awesome and killing it!

The first interview I did was one of the early morning breakfast shows. I had to stay up north and wake up at something ridiculous like 5 or 6am to get over to the studio, meet the team, go through hair and make-up, and finally do my 6-minute live interview. I remember sitting **backstage** beforehand, **watching** the show on a little TV screen in front of me. I leant over to one of the snazzy headset-wearing producers next to me and asked how **many people were watching at the moment and to be honest, I probably** shouldn't have! I thought it'd be a few hundred thousand, maybe **a million...nope!**

Apparently over 9.5 million!
Over 9 million people
were about to watch
me LIVE. I was used to
being on camera, but I
can choose what goes into
my videos and if I mess
up, I can edit that bit
out.

Walking onto the set as they were on a
commercial break, I met the two presenters who were so
friendly and relaxed, it instantly calmed me down. The
show started back up, we all got chatting and before I
knew it, my six minutes were up and I was off on the
train home! From that point, live TV didn't scare me
at all, looking back on it, it couldn't have been better.
Nowadays I can relax a little because I'll never be as
nervous as when I first appeared in front of so many people!

The press didn't stop there. That week I went from
TV shows, to radio shows, to photoshoots... to
literally everything! You name a magazine/tv
show/radio show and I was on it! It was
unbelievable. Everyone I new back at home in
Brighton was texting me saying they'd just seen
me on this or that and again, it's
something I'll never forget.

GROWING OLDER iS aND always WILL BE WEIRD FOR ME.

I remember when my cousin James turned 21 and I thought, jeez, my cousin is an adult now! He's so old... like a grown up! I also remember my sister turning 21 and kinda thinking the same and yet I don't know why, I just never imagined myself becoming an adult.

I think, deep down inside, I'm still 18... actually no, only sometimes. I can be mature when I need to be – like in meetings and for business stuff – but then I love to mess about, jump up and down on hotel beds, when they're freshly made and prank call people. But maybe that's not being 'young', that's just the kind of person you are, and I'm immature sometimes. Which I think is a good fun thing to be!

I dunno what I really planned to write on this page, I just find it so weird that I'm growing older, yet I don't feel any older if that makes sense? Do you feel the same?

My 21st birthday was amazing. My family rented a room in one of my favourite restaurants and filled the place with awesome decorations, such as personlised placemats (made by my mum!) which included pictures of me at various stages of my young life. It felt like yesterday that I was celebrating turning 16... and yet now all of a sudden I'm 22!

What. How. When?

MOVING IN WITH ZOE

Moving house is a big deal. Whether that's your family moving, moving to university, moving in with a friend or in this case, for me, moving from living by myself to living with my girlfriend!

Zoe moved down to Brighton about a year ago into a flat on the beach and I had my own flat about 15 minutes walk away.

At first this was perfect, we could both work from our own flats and then spend the evening together, but still have our own space. Space for me is really important, don't get me wrong, I love hanging out with friends and family, but I do also love spending time to myself listening to music and working without anyone disturbing me.

However, as much as we loved spending tons of time together, the fact that we had separate flats complicated things hugely!

So as you've guessed, we decided to move in together!

When the day finally came for us to move in together we were both so, so excited! Everything went to plan and before we knew it, it was like we'd never lived separately.

MY NEW YORK BOOK SIGNING!

My American book publishers offered to fly me out to New York to do a load of press along with a massive book signing in New York and, of course, I didn't turn it down. So before I knew it, Maddie (one of my managers) and I jumped on a plane and we were on our way to the big ol' city of New York!

*wait... I'm forgetting something··· or **someone***

I thought, since my mum had never been to New York before, it'd be really nice to have her come along and see what it's like to have days full of TV, radio and magazine/newspaper interviews, as well as attend her first event where people who watch my videos come to see me in person. So I booked her a ticket to come and join in!

And before we knew it, we were on a plane and on our way to **the Big Apple!** I've been very fortunate with all the traveling I've been able to do for YouTube but one thing I'd never done before was fly first class!

This was both my mum's first time and my own first time, and to say we ~~were~~ were excited would be an understatement. Only five years before I was making my first little YouTube video in my bedroom with my family camera stacked on a pile of books, and now here I was flying first class with my mum to New York to meet thousands of people who were coming to show their support for my very first book... what the heck?!!

We made the absolute most out of that flight! I spent the entire time lying flat down (because I could) and eating everything I was offered whilst watching films non-stop haha!

As soon as we landed we were picked up by one of those big blacked-out American cars (I have no idea what they're called... but the fancy-looking ones) and whisked off to do TV interviews! American press is so much fun! They're so ~~supportive~~ supportive and interested in young people who manage to turn a hobby into a job... whereas the UK press just like to ask questions about how much money you earn and whether making YouTube videos even counts as a job... stupid I know.

We only had a few days in New York, so crammed as much in for my mum to see and do as possible! She loved it!!

I never really knew what to expect with the signing – whether people in New York would be interested enough to actually come and queue up to get their book signed. I mean I knew a LOT of people came along to the signing in London, but I had no idea about New York! Yeahhhh, I was wrong as usual. There were thousands of people! But this time everything went super-smoothly and it was so, so, so much fun. I posed for pictures, chatted to fans and signed loads of books. My mum even stood next to me hugging and chatting to most people haha! It was sooo cute.

I always come away from trips wishing it carried on forever – wishing that I could spend every day with those who watch my videos.

People often ask me if I get tired during meet and greets. I can see why they'd ask as I've done some crazy stints – like eight hour ones before with no breaks – but I never really do.

The reason is because everyone I meet is always so excited, happy and upbeat, which keeps my energy so high, making me excited and chatty. It's like hanging out with tons of friends at once; it's so lovely. New York was seriously amazing and it was even better being able to fly my mum out and have her experience everything with me!

SCAN HERE

185

BaND AiD

One of the craziest things I've been involved with was Band Aid. Like actual Band Aid!

Myself, Zoe and Joe turned up to the recording studio, jumped out of our car to see tons and tons of fans and paparazzi flooding the street. How anyone knew where the recording was taking place I'll never know... but I suppose fans and paps are like detectives, they work out everything!

Whilst doing a few interviews with the press before going inside, everyone started going crazy! I turned my head to see Harry Styles rush past me and run straight inside. Things were about to get real.

All attendees were previously told not to bring any management or security, which confused me because it's not even possible to get close to some of the celebrities who were participating, due to the crazy amount of security around them 24/7.

We walked inside and went straight into the green room where everyone singing on the single was relaxing. It was so surreal. Meeting people you've frequently seen on TV, posters and in music videos in person is weird! It's hard to picture celebrities as real people, but in the green room were some of the most famous people in the world with absolutely no security — just relaxing and chatting to each other.

After chatting to Nick Grimshaw for a while, Zoe, Joe and I grabbed some snacks and sat down at a little round table because we didn't really know many other people. 'Do you want a coffee?' I felt a hand on my shoulder and turned around to say 'no thank you' to see it was Ed Sheeran... Ed was offering to make me a coffee haha!... what was happening?! He sat down at our table and we all spoke about music, YouTube and touring for about 20 minutes before heading into the studio to record the actual track.

I should probably point out that because we're not exactly singers, Zoe, Joe and I were only in the chorus of the song! We were asked to be involved by Bob Geldof who had heard that our videos were popular and decided that he wanted us to be involved to try help raise as much awareness and money for the cause.

Recording the chorus only took about 20 minutes, with everyone huddled up singing away. The entire day was so surreal for so many different reasons.

I feel so lucky and **honoured** to be able to say I've helped an amazing cause with so many talented and inspiring people.

187

I BELIEVE THERE ARE TWO KINDS OF FAMILIES IN THIS WORLD:

Cat families and dog families.

Growing up I was in a cat family. We've had cats ever since I can remember. Wait! I'm making my family sound weird: we're not like some crazy cat family — we only own two cats! My dad and I always wanted a dog, but I guess since both my parents worked full time, it wouldn't have really been fair to get a dog and then leave it home alone all day whilst Poppy and I were at school and Mum and Dad were at work.

With YouTube being our full-time jobs and enabling us to work from anywhere at anytime, Zoe and I were lucky enough to get a dog!! I sometimes think having a dog at my age isn't the most normal thing haha — but I just saw it as my chance to finally get myself a little companion. So after months and months of persuading both my parents (you'll find out why in a minute, keep reading) and Zoe that it was the best idea ever, I managed to breakthrough to them and they agreed!

(I still have no idea how I actually managed to persuade them haha).

My mum planned on cutting down on work by working fewer days per week and it was also coming up to my dad's birthday. So not only were Zoe and I in the position to get a little puppy, so were my mum and dad (kinda). They just didn't know they were, haha! I didn't keep my idea as a surprise, because a dog isn't really something they could return if they didn't agree with my 'amazing' birthday present. Persuading my dad was easy – all I had to do was ask him and he was sold on the idea! My mum, however, was a little more difficult, but with the help of my dad, we got there in the end.

The breed. A few of my friends have got pugs and if you've ever spent more than one second with a pug, you know what it's like. You walk away wanting one more than anything you've ever wanted before! What's better than one pug? Two pugs haha!! How amazing would it be if Zoe and I were to get a little female pug and my mum and dad were to get her little brother? 'So amazing' is the answer. So that's exactly what we did.

Nala and Buzz.

Nala

Don't get me wrong, I knew looking after and training a puppy would be a big challenge and completely change my life within a second. I was well aware of that from the countless books Zoe and I read up on before the puppy arrived. But words cannot describe how much work a puppy is!!

I thought I was aware... yeah... I wasn't at all.

Imagine having a little baby who runs around ALL day and can't wear a nappy... that's a puppy: pooing everywhere and eating everything, haha! Oh and I should also mention *the no sleeping part*... I had to spend every night sleeping next to her; otherwise she wouldn't sleep and would just cry. Yeah, that too.

Having said that, things did get better within a matter of weeks. Each day that passed was easier and easier, but damn, if you ever think you're ready for a puppy... you're not. But once you're put in the position and you've purchased your little companion, you have to make yourself ready – that's the only option.

I suppose that's what it must be like when you have children. You're never really 'ready' until the baby's born and then you make yourself ready.

I wouldn't change anything about Nala; she's my little friend. I love her so much! I know people who have dogs often say weird things, like they 'talk' to their dog, or that their dog can tell when they're not having a great day, but trust me it's true.
The bond between me and Nala is the best. I want her with me at all time.

...Unless she's being naughty, which is quite often. She's a crazy little one!

The Pointless Book went down better than I could have ever imagined! **My viewers went crazy** for it, resulting in the book staying at number #1 in the charts for 17 weeks... little did they know I'd been working my butt off on The Pointless Book 2! Filled with similar kinda things, my aim for the sequel was to develop popular pages from the first book and to simply make it better than the first.

The book sold like crazy! I think it did even better than first one did in the first few weeks of its publication, which was mad! And just like with the first book, before I could even blink I had finished my UK book tour and was on a plane to America and Canada.

Touring is intense because the viewers know where I'm going to be every second of the day — they know when I'm at the airport, which hotel I'm staying in, they even work **out which restaurant** I'm eating at!

The crowds are everywhere — it's like a crazy rollercoaster of non-stop meeting people.

As I'm sure I've said at some point throughout this book so far, I love meeting those who watch my videos! There's nothing quite like being able to say thank you for everything in person.

The opportunity to do this with viewers who live literally on the other side of the world is crazy.

I love being on tour and it's so much fun meeting different people across all the cities I visited. It's hard, though, for people watching my videos, because I'm so busy each day that my daily vlogs tend to become kinda similar. So with the America and Canada tour, I made sure I was able to do lots of fun activities in each city I went to.

Toronto

I discovered poutine while walking down Queen Street and I cannot even describe to you how good that stuff is! England NEEDS more poutine. Oh and we also walked on the scary glass floor at the top of the CN Tower.

Atlanta

Maddie (my manager) and I set ourselves the challenge of going to the gym at least every other day, but we kinda failed.

In Atlanta we were staying in a crazy-lovely hotel with an amazing gym. Whilst getting changed to go out, I noticed a spa treatment booklet and if you know me, you know I love a good massage — but I'm yet to find one where I haven't fallen asleep in the first five minutes. Although I think that's a good sign because it means I'm super-relaxed, right?

Anyways, I called up the spa and booked both of us in for full body massages under the condition that we go to the gym at least once, haha.
Maddie and I ~~always~~ have an ongoing joke about something weird that ALWAYS happens to me when I get a massage.

If you've never experienced getting a professional massage before, they usually light candles around the room and put a warm flannel on your face before they start the actual massage. Well except with me. And again, I have no idea why this always happens to me... but it does and Maddie LOVES to laugh about it.

So we both go off into separate rooms with our masseurs and the man massaging me doesn't just put the flannel on my face... but begins to rub my legs and feet with it... **literally like he is washing me!** I had a shower before going down to the spa to receive the massage, so it's not like I was dirty or anything!

The massage finishes and I walk into the little **waiting room where Maddie's** waiting for me and I ask if her masseur **used a flannel. She looks really confused and** says she doesn't believe me. I told her it happened again — the whole flannel thing! (I think this story is the kinda one where you have to be there for it to be funny, but trust me we ~~while~~ were dying with laughter). So now, **every time a massage is mentioned,** Maddie laughs and says something like 'it's time for your wash!' We **also went on a Segway tour, which** was so much fun! I'd never been on one before and came off of the 2.5 hour tour **wanting to buy** one so so bad...

until I realised they're like **£6,000, or something** crazy. They're the best thing ever for lazy people like me, haha!

Boston

Harvard University was a million times more impressive than I had ever imagined it to be. I know I never went to uni, but I swear it was the most typical American movie-looking uni I've ever seen! If I did go to uni, I would have loved to go to Harvard. Not just because it's Harvard haha, but because the architecture and grounds were so beautiful.

New York

Poppy's birthday was during my time in New York so I thought it would be amazing to fly her and Sean (her boyfriend) out to spend some time with us.

I booked them flights that landed a few days before I arrived in the city and into the same hotel as me, and then we all flew back a few days later, making their stay just over a week.

Neither of them had been to New York before and I knew they were going to be obsessed! Every day Poppy would call me to tell me about all the exciting things they were getting up to and all the food they were eating, haha. I **landed in New York and went straight to their hotel room** to say hello! It was so crazy seeing my sister on the other side of the world. **We had so much fun, including going to a super-fun Japanese** restaurant where they cooked all the food in front of you at your table. Oh and don't let me forget the meal out with Joey Graceffa too; I love that boy!

Basically I had the best 10 days ever. I met thousands and thousands of people who watched my videos, travelled **throughout America and did some amazingly fun things** with such good friends and family!

Growing up I never even imagined I'd be able to visit America before being a proper adult **(being 22 doesn't count, I still feel like I'm 18).** YouTube has allowed me to do the most crazy things!

A day doesn't pass by where I don't sit and think about how lucky I am to be able to do this and call it my job.

My good friend Jim Chapman had recently become engaged to his soon-to-be-wife Tanya Burr and do you know what that meant?

STAG DO!

Around eight of us jumped on a plane to France for a snowboarding trip for a few days. I should point out how incredibly hard it is to get that many YouTubers together at the SAME time. I can't even begin to tell you how many crap jokes were made by Leon on that trip... don't ever listen to anything that comes out that guy's mouth haha!

In fact, most of the words that came out of any of our mouths during the trip were either rubbish insults at each other, or daring each other to do stupid things, such as walk the entire way home naked... yeah I'll ~~know~~ leave you to work out who that was!

Don't get me wrong, the snowboarding was awesome,

I even ended up buying a snowboard on the last day. Yeah I know, kinda stupid to buy one on the LAST day. Nice one Alfie. The best part was just hanging out with the guys and the opportunity to spend proper quality time all together. Yeah we see each other at events and meetings, but it's not the same as when all the boys are together.

Out on the snow we messed about so much — daring each other to try stupid tricks and jumps where 99% of the time we ended up with our butts slamming on the ice.

Caspar was the funniest: **he literally doesn't care at all and goes for anything you tell** him to, which he somehow manages to pull off (and it's sick!)! He's even better than Marcus, who likes to think of himself as a **pro hahahaha!**

Wait how did I nearly forget about Leon crashing a wedding in a bar we were in **and spending the entire evening dancing with them?! Leon's hips are like no other. As soon as he hears a song he likes there's no stopping him!** He's an animal on the dance floor and let's just say I felt **sorry for the bride and** groom because he KILLED it with every move you can imagine.

Jimbo if you're reading this, **thanks for such** an amazing **time and congratulations again to you and Tan x**

SCAN HERE

IT'S CRAZY HOW YOUR LIFE CAN FLASH BEFORE YOUR VERY EYES.

I remember being 11 years old and wishing I was 16 so I could stay up later in the evenings and do the fun things teenagers can do. Now here I am at 22 not knowing where the time has gone! Don't wish anything away; enjoy every moment you have!

It's absolutely mad to think that I've now been doing YouTube for six years... what even?! Where has the time gone? It feels like yesterday that I put my family

camera on a little stack of books and DVDs in my bedroom and filmed my first video. It feels like yesterday that I hit **100 subscribers**, **1,000 subscribers** and now somehow **4,000,000 subscribers.**

There aren't many negatives about making videos for YouTube as a full-time job. **Well actually that's not true!** There is one thing that sometimes does get a little tricky and that's being able to stop 'working'. ~~I~~ I love what I do so damn much; I want to create videos all day every day and **when other things get in the way, such as dentist appointments etc, I don't want to go to them haha!**

I find it really hard to sleep at night. My head's buzzing with different video ideas and I just want to jump up and go film/edit. To be honest I kinda wish humans didn't have to sleep so I could get more done each day.

Separating 'work' and 'non-work' time is so hard when you love what you do, so I decided to create a fun and inspiring area where **I could to go and 'work' each day, which will help me cr**eate even better content. I searched online for months and months until I found the perfect office not too far from my house. The feel and look is like nothing I've seen in Brighton before. The shape and style is sooo me, I became obsessed and had to rent it even if it was much bigger than I needed.

I'm not too great at planning or **waiting for things.**

I'm used to filming a video, editing and uploading it within a day or two, so anything that takes longer than a few days really bugs me. **Poppy's so, so good at planning, organising and designing things, that was literally** her job after uni, designing an art studio and planning where each piece of art goes etc. We sat down on the floor in my new office with pen, **paper and a tape measure and** planned out what we needed and what was going to go where.

We smashed it in one day.

I've been asked a few times why I need an office if I'm just filming videos. But what people don't realise is how nice it can be to leave an office and **to actually go home.**

There are **tons** of meetings and boring bits I have to do – **it's not all just creating fun videos** (even though it looks like that), so being able to ~~to~~ leave the meetings behind and arrive home where no work, or only fun work happens, is super-nice. **But it's more than that: as you know I love buying weird gadgets and toys, so being able to build an office** with a table tennis table and other cool things inspires me and keeps my videos fun and stupid like they've always been since day one.

It's also nice having somewhere dedicated to filming. Before, **when I wanted to film a sit-down vlog or challenge, I'd have to tidy up our bedroom and make it look all nice to film in;** now I've got somewhere that is only used for filming, which is so much more efficient and allows me to film more regularly (and doesn't **disturb Zoe or Nala!**).

203

So many exciting projects have months and months of work that go into them before anyone can even know that they're going on and an amazing example of this is our Zalfie wax figures at Madame Tussauds London!

When leaving Madame Tussauds, you're asked for your most wished-for Celebrity waxwork and somehow Zoe and I were the most-requested people in 2015?!

Crazy I know, don't ask me how or why, I don't understand it!

We received an email asking us if we'd like to be put into the wax museum, which only adds a couple of new people each year. My initial response was like what? how? why? when? huh? What's going on? I can't go in Madame Tussauds...I just make little YouTube videos; I'm not a celebrity!

But once the Madame Tussauds team explained that it's literally done on whoever is the most requested that year, it made me sit back and think about why we were even considering turning this opportunity down! If people were telling Madame Tussauds they wanted us there, why would I say no to that?

Zoe and I spent days and days in different studios doing photoshoots – sat in the strangest of positions for hours on end whilst being spun around. We even took Nala along to some of the shoots to sit with us whilst we were being measured up. At one point I was sat in my boxers for literally 6 hours with some-one measuring every single part of my body, with

tiny stickers stuck all over me to help calculate the distances.

I'm super-fussy about what my hair looks like each day, let alone an entire w**ax figure of ME! Each pie**ce of hair is hand-pressed into my wax head and dyed/trimmed to look like mine. Layers and layers of paint and make-up was put on my body and face to match my own skin colour... The work that was put into making my figure was ridiculous!

The big day was here! Zoe and I could finally tell our audiences what we'd been working on secretly for so long! Annnd we could also finally see Zoe and I in actual Madame Tussauds in London in our remade bedroom, looking as though we were vlogging!

All of our friends and family came down for the grand opening and it was just crazy to see so much support for such a surreal opportunity.

Each and every day I get so many messages from people sending pictures of 'me' with them, when in fact it's them and my wax figure! I love that they can kinda get to meet me any day of the year, **even when I'm** busy and at **home.**

205

I feel like I'm going to regret writing this because, knowing me, I'm going to forget something or someone, so I'm sorry if I've forgotten you! Let's take a step back and look at just how many amazing things my friends have all achieved.

I've written a lot a about me, but my close YouTube friends are taking over the world and I'm so, so proud of them!

Marcus: A book. SourcedBox (yum!). Music video and song.

Zoe: Two bestselling books. A product line. 10 million subscribers. A wax figure in Madame Tussauds.

Joe: A bestselling graphic novel. A film.

Connor Franta: A book. A new creative company.

Troye: EP wild. Debut album Blue Neighbourhood.

Louise: A chart-topping book. A diary. A clothing line.

Dan and Phil: A book. App.

Chai: Moved to London and traveled to tons of countries.

Niomi: SourcedBox (yum!).

Tyler: A crazy-good book. A podcast. Merchandise.
A tour. A documentary.

Joey: An awesome book. Crazy (and I mean crazy)
good shorts (films not actually shorts haha!).

Jim: Stationery line. Merchandise. TV presenting.

Poppy: A blog, which is killing it!!

Tanya: An amazing book. A product line.

Caspar: A film. Merchandise.

...and so so many more!

JUST REALISED I HAVEN'T REALLY WRITTEN ENOUGH ABOUT HOW SUPPORTIVE ALL MY NON-YOUTUBE FRIENDS IN BRIGHTON ARE ABOUT MY YOUTUBE VIDEOS, AND THE FACT THAT I'M BUSY 99% OF THE TIME AND NOT ABLE TO SEE THEM AS OFTEN AS I'D LIKE TO.

Going to get a little deep for a second now: hanging out with people who don't create YouTube videos can often be a little bit tricky because they want to know so much about what I'm up to and how it's all going, that sometimes it feels like I'm being interviewed. I know for sure they don't mean it; they're just interested to know how I've been and what I've been doing. But it can often be a little intense, and as odd as it sounds, as I make videos about my life every day... I don't actually really like to talk about myself. So I find it weird when friends spend the time we have together talking about me. I often have to work really hard to move the conversation away from myself and onto other topics.

But my friends from back at school — you guys know who you are, are always so amazing and ignore all the YouTube stuff and just chill and have fun whilst we're hanging out!

I THOUGHT I WAS GOING TO DIE

The crazy thing about making friends with people online is that you can know them so well from tweeting/texting and watching their videos, but you may not have actually met them in real life.

This is exactly what happened with me, Roman and Britt: we'd chatted online for ages, but since they live in America and I live in the UK it was nearly impossible for us to spend time together.

We got DM'ing late one night on Twitter to see if we were all free to hang out. Bear in mind that messaging each other was a little ~~difficult~~ difficut due to the time difference.

I woke up with a message from Roman saying he was free over the next week... no notice – literally the week we were **texting haha! And somehow, by chance, so was I!**

I love to be spontaneous, but I've never done something quite like what I did next. I went online there and then and booked flights for the next morning super-early and then messaged him to say **I'm coming to stay for the next 5 days haha!** I kinda even forgot to tell my friends. Zoe knew, of course, because she was going to have to look after Nala and I think I also told my family, but before I knew it I was at the airport.

Five minutes later I received a call from my manager asking me **if I was around the next day for a meeting**

and I suddenly realised I hadn't even told my management I was going! I had quite a ~~few~~ few meetings in my diary for that **week (including writing this book!)** so kinda had to break the news that I was about to fly to America...**and was already in the airport haha.**

I'd never flown alone before, but I like time to myself so I thought, if anything, I'd enjoy it **and just relax.** After a quick change-over in Chicago, I hopped on the smallest plane I've ever seen in my life... honestly I thought I wasn't going to make it.

First of all the plane was the size of a tiny private jet, **minus the luxury insides haha! I think there were 7 or 12 people on the flight and we were** ALL sitting right near the front... now me being super-observant of everything ever, **I clocked onto this straight away and just assumed more passengers must be coming on any second.** Welllllllll... that was until the one air hostess on board closed the tiny little plane door and noted on **a piece of tissue that we were all there.**

A PIECE OF TISSUE. Not even paper!

She looked a little confused and then told us that the plane might be flying with **its nose pointing**

down, which is why we were all at the front.

I WANTED TO GET OFF *OF THE PLANE.*

I honestly felt like it wasn't even worth the risk! Why was I on this? **Was Roman pranking me?** I spent most of the flight listening to a calming app on my phone **with my head in my hands.**

A plane journey has never gone so slowly in my life. It was meant to be 1 hour and 30 minutes, but for some reason and don't even ask me why, it only took 50 minutes! Maybe all the weight at the front made us fly faster hahaha.

Arriving at the airport to see viewers waiting for me was so refreshing! I could ~~speak~~ speak to people about my weird near-death experience.

Walking outside I could see Roman and Britt's MASSIVE (and I mean *MASSIVE*) red pick-up style truck. I hopped in and it was like we'd known each for years! Well I guess we did, but had just never met before.

Spending a few days in a completely **different environment,** laughing at all the differences we had and trying new things, was crazy. It's not often I get to travel without meetings, book signings **or YouTube meet** ups. Saying that, we kept ourselves busy. I swear we did more in those few days than I usually do in a month! But more importantly I came away with two amazing new friends who I know will be staying with me in the UK some time soon and that excites me so much.

I came away feeling so refreshed and inspired to create better videos than ever before. Both Roman and Britt's love of vlogging is like nothing I've ever seen.

They're both so engaged with their audience and spend all day, every day making sure their videos are as fun and entertaining as possible. Honestly it made me sit back and reminded me why I'm doing YouTube and showed me why I love it so damn much.

Big thanks to Roman and Britt for making my stay so much fun and for welcoming me into their home. Oh and don't let me forget Kane the master of the Lego game, with whom I we spent hours playing on the Playstation haha!

Keeping motivated in life is one of the most important things. If you don't love what you do, you need to do everything to change that. No one should accept working a job they don't enjoy. I'm not saying quit your job and play video games every day and expect it to become your job. But what I mean is: spend ALL your spare time working your butt off on doing what you LOVE. What's the worst that can happen? You finish work at 5pm, but you can spend all your spare time enjoying yourself. And the best? The best that can happen is when your passion, your hobby, your dream job becomes reality, and all of your hard work outside of work has enabled you to gradually finish the original job you disliked and you can now focus on what you LOVE.

This is one of my favourite quotes of all time:

'If you don't build your own dream, someone else will hire you to help build theirs.'
— Tony Gaskins

Annd this pretty much brings me up to today January 20th 2016. I'm currently sat in my office spending most of my days in meetings, filming/editing videos and planning new, exciting projects.

This year is purely about videos. I want to put 99% of my time and effort into creating the best videos I possibly can. It's far too easy to be carried away by the amazing opportunities, but I always like to remind myself of the most important thing in every situation and if my videos drop in quality, then those opportunities won't be available any longer.

Last year I often left filming videos to the very last minute. I'd end up filming/editing and uploading all in one day, which resulted in a few rushed videos, me being really stressed and meant I had tons of issues with my chest. Don't worry the pains are sorted now!

So yeah, this year I'm planning all my videos way in advance (as much as possible haha!) and I'm going to be so on top of all my work! So far 2016 is going very well. I've got so many exciting things planned and I can't wait for my audience to hear about them!

2016 IS going to be the best year of my life so far.

I WANT TO TRAVEL THE WORLD.

All my college friends took gap years to go to places such as Thailand, Vietnam, Australia and China, but because I was busy working on YouTube stuff, I never got the chance to properly travel. Don't get me wrong, I've seen a lot of the world – via different YouTube events, book signings, **meet ups** – but I haven't done any backpacking or any REAL travelling where I'm not sat in a hotel 90% of the time.

This year I want to pack a big bag full of camera equipment and go travelling! Whether that means planning an awesome adventure with friends or even going to the airport with a friend and buying a ticket for the next available flight (and not knowing where we're going until the last minute or how we're even going to get home!). The thought of that excites me so much and I really want to make it happen!

'ALFIE YOU'RE 22 AND YOU HAVEN'T GOT A DRIVER'S LICENCE... COME ON!'

...is what everyone around me is saying, haha! I WILL pass my driving test this year.

I will. I will. I will.

As I'm sure you've gathered by now, putting my life online is literally my life. I wake up every day looking forward to creating videos and talking to those who watch them. However this year I think it'll be important for me to have the odd week offline every now and again for holidays with my family, or visiting friends who don't make YouTube videos. I had my first proper break, a week off at the end of 2015 and it was so crazy! Not filming my life was so surreal: at first I didn't enjoy not filming, then after three days I felt so relaxed about not having to worry about having the time to edit and upload, or if the internet is even going to be good enough to upload.

There's so much that goes into daily vlogging and I often feel that the viewers see the 15 minute video and forget how much time/effort goes into those videos seven days a week, 365 days a year... Let alone making another eight videos a week on top of that, like I do! But yeah, this year I think I'm going to try have a few days offline every now and again just to make sure I'm living in the moment and fully enjoy everything I'm doing in life.

THANK YOU!

I've never once thrown away a letter or card that a viewer has given me. They're stored in boxes and boxes and boxes in my parents' house, my house and even my office, and this year I'd love to take some time out to sit down and read through them. There's such an overwhelming amount that I don't think it'd even be possible to read them all in a year, haha! I'll probably read a few each day until I'm like 80 or something. Reading them can be my little pick-me-up each ~~every~~ morning. Some people need their morning coffee to get them up and ready for the day haha, but I'll be reading my 'fan' mail to get me up and ready!

Seriously though, I appreciate all the time and effort that everyone has put into the cards and letters, and for sure I will read them all at some point don't you worry!

This also ties in with press work. I've done so many amazing photoshoots and interviews, but often don't get time to actually take in how crazy it all is. Luckily my mum tries to purchase everything I'm in and is turning it all into a scrapbook for me to look back on. So maybe starting this year, or next year, I'll start reading through it all and reflect on all the amazing things I'm lucky enough to be able to have done so far on this journey.

I can't even begin to describe how fortunate and lucky I feel to have done so many amazing things at the age of 22 **and it's only because of YOU** reading this. You've honestly **made my dreams** come true... wait, not even my dreams. I would never have even dreamt about some of the things that have happened to me!

I have so much to thank **my family for! They've** always ways been so, so incredibly supportive and are always there if I ever need advice or help with anything and for sure *this doesn't go unnoticed!* **Mum, Dad** and Pop you guys are the best family I could have asked **for!**

What I've managed to achieve is something you could easily do yourself. **You reading this could easily be in my position experiencing the same things** I have and I don't want you to forget that. I'm not anything special.

I'm just a normal person **who's had some not-so-normal things** happen in my life so far. Don't EVER let anyone tell you **that you're not good enough. Spend** every hour of every day proving to them that you are!

Never settle for less than you deserve!

n't know where my future is going to lead me, but what I do know is that I'd love for you to carry on this journey with me as I know it's going to be a fun one! We've ~~achieved~~ achieved so much together so far and I honestly believe that it's only just begun. I'm only 22 so there's a lot more to experience and go through together. Let's plan some amazing and crazy stuff and hopefully I'll even get to meet you in person along the way.

I've spent so many hours in bed, in my office, on the sofa, on trains... literally anywhere I could writing this scrapbook and I don't know whether to be sad that it's coming to an end or happy that I've enjoyed looking back on everything so much.

This book is a piece of me. Each page freezes a moment of my life in time. I hope you've found the weird little stories from throughout my life interesting... and if you didn't then at least I will when I look back at it in years to come haha!

Alfie xx

22nd January 2016

PS - I passed my driving test 1st time, didn't I!